THE JEWISH QUARTERLY

The Jewish Quarterly is published four times a year
by The Jewish Quarterly Pty Ltd

Publisher: Morry Schwartz

ISBN 9781922517173 E-ISBN 9781743823064
ISSN 0449010X E-ISSN 23262516

ALL RIGHTS RESERVED.
No part of this publication may be reproduced, stored in a retrieval system
or transmitted in any form by any means electronic, mechanical, photocopying,
recording or otherwise without the prior consent of the publishers.

Essays and reviews © retained by the authors

Subscriptions 1 year print & digital (4 issues): £42 GBP | $56 USD.
1 year digital only: £25 GBP | $32 USD. Payment may be made
by Mastercard or Visa. Payment includes postage and handling.

Subscribe online at jewishquarterly.com or email subscribe@jewishquarterly.com
Correspondence should be addressed to: The Editor, The Jewish Quarterly,
22–24 Northumberland Street, Collingwood VIC 3066 Australia
Phone +61 3 9486 0288 Email enquiries@jewishquarterly.com

The Jewish Quarterly is published under licence from the
Jewish Literary Trust Limited, which exercises a governance function.

UK Company Number: 01189861. UK Charity Commission Number: 268589.

Directors of the Jewish Literary Trust: Lance Blackstone (chair),
John Cohen, Andrew Renton and Michael Strelitz.

Founding Editor: Jacob Sonntag.

Editor: Jonathan Pearlman. Associate Editor: Jo Rosenberg. Literary Editor:
Natasha Lehrer. Management: Elisabeth Young. Design: John Warwicker and
Tristan Main. Production: Marilyn de Castro. Typesetting: Tristan Main.

Cover image: Natacha Pisarenko / Associated Press
Image on p.vi: Alejandro Pagni / AP Images

Issue 252, May 2023
THE JEWISH QUARTERLY

Contributors ... v

Javier Sinay (translated by Robert Croll)
The AMIA bombing ... 1

History
Ian Black Madrid, 1991: When enemies finally met ... 67

Community
Rena Molho Remembering Salonica,
capital of the Diaspora ... 75

Reviews
James McAuley Justice and the Holocaust ... 80

Samantha Ellis The books of Ruth ... 88

Mark Glanville Pinning down Joseph Roth ... 95

Contributors

Ian Black (1953–2023) was a journalist at *The Guardian* and a visiting senior fellow at the Middle East Centre of the London School of Economics. He wrote several books, including *Enemies and Neighbours: Arabs and Jews in Palestine and Israel, 1917–2017*.

Robert Croll is an artist and translator based in Chicago. His translations include Hebe Uhart's *Animals* and the three volumes of Ricardo Piglia's *The Diaries of Emilio Renzi*.

Samantha Ellis is the author of *How to Be a Heroine* and *Take Courage: Anne Brontë and the Art of Life*. Her plays include *How to Date a Feminist* and *Cling to Me Like Ivy*.

Mark Glanville is a writer and singer. His work includes the memoir *The Goldberg Variations* and the recital *Barbaric Verses*, which debuted in London in February 2023.

James McAuley is a contributing columnist at *The Washington Post* and the author of *The House of Fragile Things: Jewish Art Collectors and the Fall of France*.

Rena Molho is the co-founder of the Society for the Study of Greek Jewry, and has taught Greek Jewish history at Panteion University. She lives in Salonica.

Javier Sinay is a recipient of the Gabriel García Márquez Award and the author of *The Murders of Moisés Ville: The Rise and Fall of the Jerusalem of South America*. He lives in Buenos Aires.

The AMIA bombing

Javier Sinay
(translated by Robert Croll)

1.

There is a great crowd of police, among them snipers and armoured trucks; there are green and blue uniforms and private security guards questioning everyone who reaches the metal detectors, and when my turn comes the question is: "How did you hear about today's event?" Which seems slightly outrageous: everyone knows it is happening today.

It was not easy to reach the exact site of the terrorist attack memorial event. The stage is set up on Calle Pasteur – in the centre of Buenos Aires, where shops and offices abound, buses roar and motorbikes hum – but the surrounding area has been closed off to vehicles and, in some places, fenced off to foot traffic.

I respond briefly, then receive a banner displaying the photo of one of the victims from the attack. On the back I read her story:

> Aída Mónica Feldman de Goldfeler is 39 years old. She is married to Mario and has two children: Juan and Gabriela. She enjoys painting and decorative arts, and she studied at the School

of Fine Arts. She is a happy woman, always making jokes, and does what she can to help her family. On Monday, 18 July 1994, she leaves home early to do some paperwork. As times are hard, she is taking the opportunity to stop by the AMIA and register herself at the Job Center.

Goldfeler – who looks weary in the portrait, with dark circles under her eyes – was waiting her turn when the attack occurred.

The photos of dozens of victims have been handed out in the street. This sea of motionless grey faces proliferating in our hands evokes the famous demonstrations for the *desaparecidos* of the 1976 dictatorship. A helicopter cuts through the sky and ambulances arrive; even the director-general of the emergency services has come. Alberto Crescenti is a man of action who puts himself on the frontlines alongside the paramedics when there is a train accident or a nightclub fire, and who, this morning, will come to the aid of an elderly woman when she collapses in a moment of grief.

Today is Monday, 18 July 2022: after two years of pandemic, during which mass activities were suspended, this annual gathering to demand justice has assembled once more. There are some 6000 people, a restless, expansive crowd, and the sound of a million footfalls is like a threatening whisper.

These people are demanding a resolution to the attack on the AMIA – the Argentine Israelite Mutual Association, the largest Jewish social organisation in Argentina – and that someone be brought to justice for the eighty-five victims killed and 151 injured. Given no one is in prison after all these years, there is a disquieting belief that no serious investigations occurred. This is not quite true. It was proved that at 9.53 a.m. on Monday, 18 July 1994, the AMIA building was razed to its foundations by a white Renault

Trafic van, licence plate C-1498506, carrying 300 kilograms of explosives and driven by a suicide bomber. It was proved that the masterminds were high-ranking members of the Iranian government, including one president, two ministers and an ambassador, and that Hezbollah executed the plan. But it has not been possible to confirm this in a courtroom because none of the suspects have agreed to stand trial, in Argentina or anywhere else, nor could they be captured.

And yet even after three trials, with the Supreme Court of Justice identifying it as "the most complex case in Argentine legal history", even after twenty-eight years of grief (now twenty-nine), a great deal remains unknown. There have been cover-ups. Conspiracy theories. Weak evidence. Suspicions. Alternative theories. One judge and two prosecutors removed from the case. And one prosecutor dead: Alberto Nisman, discovered in his bathroom with a bullet in his head. That is why this whispering multitude has gathered today on Calle Pasteur. The security forces put on their show and, in a society where antisemitism seems to have diminished, one cannot be sure if their deployment is a sign of the government's cooperation with the Jewish community or only a spectacle – or if there is indeed a threat that demands the presence of snipers.

At 9.53 a shocking siren blares. The event begins.

2.

"There Still May Be Dozens of People Under the Rubble": front page, *Clarín* newspaper, Buenos Aires, Tuesday, less than twenty-four hours after the attack. A catastrophic headline.

Calle Pasteur appeared quite different on 18 July 1994. The seven-storey AMIA building, a block of granite and cement from the 1940s, had crashed down upon itself with a deafening noise that many heard from several blocks away, unable to identify it but certain at once that something was wrong. (I heard it too: I was thirteen years old, finishing my breakfast; it was the winter school holidays; I turned the TV on and then everything went *boom*.)

Calle Pasteur was a chasm. Blood, panic, screaming. People running the way scared animals run. The floors had trembled, the walls had shaken, and glass had fallen from the sky like lacerating rain. What was left of the AMIA building looked like a sandcastle crushed out of scorn; rubble and debris were scattered over the entire block. The Argentine people were right back in March 1992, when a car bomb had destroyed the Israeli embassy in Buenos Aires. Sudden mass death had again invaded a regular morning in the middle of the city.

When the AMIA attack occurred there were some 120 people working inside the building – it housed the DAIA (Delegation of Argentine Israelite Associations), a Jewish umbrella organisation; the IWO (a Yiddish acronym for the Institute for Jewish Research), which housed a large library; and several other organisations. Many of the people who survived were in the rear wing. Jacobo Chemanuel, a 56-year-old maintenance worker, was in the second underground level. There in the darkness he was buried under seven metres of debris, his legs trapped by a water tank and his body covered with iron. The firefighters heard his cries and excavated a twisting tunnel towards him using saws and blowtorches, though the rescue seemed nearly impossible. Over the course of several hours they passed Chemanuel coffee, food, sedatives, saline solution and an oxygen mask. They told him he must not fall asleep, and each aid worker who came in through the tunnel offered him encouragement. Chemanuel held on inside that sarcophagus and became a source of honour – and humanity – for the rescuers. It took them thirty-one hours to bring him out. They had succeeded: he was alive.

On that first day, the paramedics counted twenty-six dead, 146 injured and seventy-four missing. Who knows how many people were out on the sidewalk in a dense commercial area like that? The AMIA looked much like wartime Beirut, or Mexico City after the 1985 earthquake: urban tragedies often have a similar appearance. The fiery wave of the blast had thrown cars into the air so that they looked like crumpled paper. Iron bars and columns were bent at astonishing angles. The neighbouring buildings were like skulls: no facades now, no residents. Urban tragedies may appear similar, but each has its own scent, and on Calle Pasteur that morning there was smoke, dust and the unpleasant odour of ammonia.

> *The first thing the judge saw was the bodies, three or four of them piled up in a corner*

In the ruins, hundreds of people were trying to assist in the rescue. At 10.30 a.m., an aid worker with a megaphone said: "When someone lifts their arms, everyone be quiet. Otherwise it will be impossible to do anything for the people who are trapped!" Juan José Galeano, the federal judge who had just been assigned to head the investigation into the case, arrived on the block along with his court secretary and two police chiefs. The first thing he saw was bodies, three or four of them piled up in a corner. One block from the epicentre of the explosion, a woman called to a policeman: "Please, officer, get that out of here!" She was pointing to the severed arm of a man, wrapped in a white shirt, but the policeman couldn't bring himself to touch it. Hours later, the police managed to organise the rescue efforts. The judge had ordered that access be restricted and, when faced with the choice between saving a life or collecting evidence, that life come first.

The experts ruled out a gas explosion and, based on damage done to buildings and cars, and the similarity to the Israeli embassy bombing, identified it as a terrorist attack. At 1.45 p.m., President Carlos Menem had a phone call with Israel's prime minister, Yitzhak Rabin, and agreed to receive disaster agents to work with Argentina's own. (Two days later, in a message on national television, Menem begged "forgiveness for this terrible incident", pledged to redouble the efforts to solve it and attempted to respond to criticism over the lack of punishment for the embassy attack.) That afternoon, a 31-year-old Iraqi citizen named Adnam Mohamed Yousif was arrested in Paso de los Libres, a town on the Brazilian border (he was taken to Buenos Aires to be interrogated but was released soon afterwards as his only infringement was an expired passport). At the same time, campaigning in Portland, United States president Bill Clinton delivered a statement: this attack would not halt negotiations for peace in the Middle East.

Soon afterwards, as the sun was setting, Menem met the director of the DAIA, Rubén Beraja, at the Government House. The rescue efforts continued perilously. At 7.42 p.m., a firefighter yelled: "It's all coming down!" He threw himself to safety and watched as an enormous section of masonry broke loose and buried ten other firefighters, injuring all of them. After the meeting with Beraja, President Menem headed to the Hospital de Clínicas, which had taken in seventy-two injured and over 700 people who wanted to donate blood. Inside, a woman with a thick stream of blood oozing from her head became aware of what had happened when she saw the medical staff attending to a man who had just lost an eye, another with his leg broken in several places and two children in a state of shock. That night there would be no silence.

3.

Jews had begun arriving in Argentina in the 1890s thanks to Baron de Hirsch, a German philanthropist who arranged for them to leave the Tsarist empire and sow the pampas. The AMIA was founded a hundred years before the attack, in 1894. Later, over the course of the twentieth century, the Jewish Colonization Association (Baron de Hirsch's company) founded some fifteen agricultural colonies: from these arose the legend of the Jewish gaucho. Argentina has perhaps the only Jewish community that began in the fields, although today the Jewish gaucho is no more than that: a legend. "We planted wheat and harvested doctors," Jewish mothers in Argentina used to say of their children – first, second or third generation – who left the colonies by the hundreds and headed for the major cities in search of a better education, modern amenities and opportunities for work.

Now the first thing you see, at the building that is the very centre of Jewish life in Argentina, is cement pillars: barriers to prevent car bombs, an adornment repeated at Jewish schools, synagogues, clubs. Next, you see the names of the eighty-five victims, inscribed on large black panels, and the security post that stands behind the pillars: an armoured door, a window with mirrored glass, a vigilant sense of *bitachon*, security. One of the guards asks for my identification and announces me on his radio. Another goes through my belongings and watches me walk through the metal detector. Once through security, you see an enormous open-air space – yet another defence. And then you see the new AMIA building, which opened in 1999: a bunker of Israeli design, solid and impenetrable, erected on the site of the original building. No terrorist could even touch the wall of this architecture.

I first came here some years ago, searching for my past: there were old documents I needed to find while investigating the origins of the Jewish community in Argentina for a book I was writing. Now I have returned, seeking answers to the tragedy of the terrorist attack. I need to understand what no one yet understands: why, after nearly thirty years, there has been no justice. What went wrong. And what we might still be able to learn. But even as my investigation begins, I know it will be a labyrinth of competing clues, operations, crimes and interests. A labyrinth in which few are seeking the truth, and in which, several times, I will lose my way.

A few minutes after I enter the building, I'm in Amos Linetzky's office, watching as he murmurs a blessing over his coffee. Unlike some leaders in the Jewish community who appear formal and aged, the AMIA president for the 2022–2025 term seems young, energetic. He comes from a family of klezmer musicians. His grandfather spoke Yiddish and played tango, something hardly surprising in a country of migrants. Linetzky, an attorney specialising in international law, doesn't dress like an Orthodox Jew, but he is one. And he is the rising star of a political party at the AMIA that everyone else – those who are not Orthodox – seems to hate.

"Just as it proves very difficult for us to explain what happened that day, it's also difficult to explain what did not happen in twenty-eight years," Linetzky said in his speech at the commemorative event in 2022. "What can explain that in twenty-eight years it has not been possible to capture even one of the many perpetrators of such a tragedy? The AMIA case is one of the most shameful reflections of Argentine history." His direct confrontation of the judiciary and political system was not bad, considering that some leaders in the Jewish community have been marked as accomplices, along with those same judicial and political authorities, in the cover-up of the attack; Rubén Beraja (the president of the DAIA in 1994) was tried and acquitted.

"The memory is part of our daily life," Linetzky tells me. Being president of the AMIA means spending hours upon hours talking about the attack, whether you like it or not. I ask him why so many security forces had been deployed at the most recent event. "Generally there's security at every Jewish event, and this is the Jewish event par excellence," he says. "I don't think there was any special reason beyond that."

> *Every president has put this drama to some political use*

In the days prior to the memorial event, President Alberto Fernández received Linetzky at the Government House. Every president has received the AMIA leader each year since 1994: the attack has always been a troubled issue of state. Every president has put this drama to some political use – and three of them ended up accused themselves.

"Reclaiming justice has been in our DNA since '94: starting in that year, the AMIA has had enormous political exposure," Linetzky continues, and as he talks I can't help noticing that his office is too organised: the bookcase with too few books, the round table spotless, the desk with no loose papers. Maybe it's because he has just begun his term. Or maybe he does not spend much time here. "The passage of time shows not only total impunity, but also a lack of preparation," he says. "Is the criminal justice system prepared to handle acts of terrorism? Why didn't the legislation adapt? These are questions that don't have answers."

Linetzky is forty-two. Maybe he'll be circling around the Jewish leadership for decades to come. And so we talk about the future of the search for justice. "I believe we can't get used to living with impunity," he says. "It's complicated …"

He takes a sip of coffee, this time in silence.

4.

Judge Juan José Galeano made his way to the morgue through a half-empty city, as if in a nightmare. It was the night of 18 July 1994 and not much time had passed since his appointment as a federal judge. The federal jurisdiction convicted politicians and wealthy criminals: it was the top level of the justice system. Galeano was a man of thirty-four who always kept his stubble a bit overgrown and wore a suit and tie as if out of obligation. He still considered himself a *cuzco*, one of the yipping dogs from the common jurisdiction where he had made his career. That jurisdiction judged not politicians but poor thieves. Galeano claimed not to have political ties but others said otherwise, and his federal judge's gavel had already fallen on some 500 cases – many for drug trafficking, some involving big fish. The AMIA case would swallow everything.

It was not yet 8 p.m. but in that austral winter, the morgue, which operated behind the old School of Medicine, appeared gloomy, in the style of a European film. The atmosphere was anarchic. Ambulances were coming and going, stretchers clattering across the floors. The man in charge, Dr Heraldo Donnewald, came out to intercept Galeano. He said they were over capacity, that this was a work holiday at the morgue, that he was about to leave on a trip himself. Dozens more bodies would be coming in the next day, but whoever planned the rosters had never imagined a moment like this.

Amid the chaos, the judge moved carefully through the rooms. The medics had set aside the corpses that had evidence of a car bomb – automobile debris – within their flesh. A shock absorber had been embedded in the torso of the doorman from one building. Another victim had been impaled by a tie rod. Of the suicide bomber no traces remained. Outside the morgue, police officers and intelligence agents were betting it had been a Renault Trafic van, as they had located a door with the rhombus logo at the scene of the massacre. Galeano ordered Donnewald to call in the absent morticians and suspend his trip.

> *The country did not recognise itself: it was a runaway train crashing into the Middle East*

The day after the attack – Tuesday – the Israelis arrived. They brought devices for detecting people under the rubble and two dogs trained to search for survivors. Before boarding the plane, Zeev Livne, the general in charge, ordered his Argentine counterpart to have cranes ready when they landed. In a brief press conference at the Ezeiza airport, General Livne said they were there to collaborate. But in the coming days the Argentine aid workers would be forced to follow their orders – and no one likes a newcomer telling them what to do in their own home.

The Israeli undersecretary of Latin American Affairs, Dov Schmorak, who had come with Livne, met with President Menem and explained Israel's hypothesis: an act of Islamist terrorism, with local support. He described it as the largest attack against Jews since World War II. It was now Wednesday, and the bombing was the only topic of conversation in Argentina. The country did not recognise itself: it was a runaway train crashing into the Middle East. Germany and the United States had already joined Israel as bodyguards for Argentina. They were thinking about Hezbollah, about Islamic Jihad, about Iran. But no one had claimed the attack.

From the depths of that smoking ossuary on Calle Pasteur, the evils and myths of Argentina would emerge. Antisemitism lurked in dark corners of the security forces. There were some who believed in the Andinia Plan, a supposed Jewish conspiracy to take Patagonia. But the hotbed was the Triple Frontier between Argentina, Paraguay and Brazil: in that jungle region, with hazy boundaries, the Islamist radicals could hide. This all existed alongside the world's fifth-largest Jewish community.

The judiciary, reformed to leave behind the methods of the dictatorship that had ended in 1983, did not have the capability for a case of this kind. Its unquestioning reliance on the intelligence services would become clear as well. The intelligence services were untrustworthy at best or, at worst, simple mercenaries. The police were no better: several times they worked to conceal their own crimes.

As Undersecretary Schmorak and President Menem were speaking, General Livne arrived on the scene at that block of Calle Pasteur. "What is the direction of street traffic?" he asked Judge Galeano. After the response, he pointed towards a pile of rubble. "The engine of the car bomb should be roughly there."

5.

In a preliminary meeting on the Friday after the bombing, agents from the Secretariat of State Intelligence (SIDE) presented a video on the 1992 Israeli embassy case to the judge, some court officials and two police chiefs. A few blocks away, the rescuers were still searching for survivors. The investigators spoke about the advances they had made (not many), handed out folders of reports, went over their conclusions and identified Hezbollah as a possible perpetrator of the embassy attack, for which the organisation had indeed claimed responsibility. Galeano believed that intelligence cooperation was essential for the AMIA investigation. The SIDE had two well-differentiated sections: Sala Patria, which dealt with domestic affairs, and Section 85, counterintelligence. Spies infiltrate terrorist cells, they share and buy information, they listen, they know. But they can also sell you out and betray you. Now the game was about to begin.

One of the SIDE chiefs approached the judge after the meeting: the Venezuelan embassy had reported that there was a relevant witness. They must go and see him urgently.

The next day – Saturday – Galeano, the two prosecutors, some SIDE officials and a few other investigators boarded one of the presidential aeroplanes and flew to Caracas, Venezuela. In the Argentine embassy a nervous man was waiting for them. Manuchehr Moatamer, the witness.

"This man escaped from an attempted kidnapping by Iranian diplomats in Venezuela," I am told by Eamon Mullen, one of the prosecutors who travelled with Galeano, now a private attorney. This is the first time he has given an in-depth interview about the case, and we talk for hours in a restaurant on the edge of the city. "I think at a certain point the truth needs to be known," he tells me. "I stayed silent for many years."

Speaking rapidly, the witness said he had worked for the Iranian government. In Ershad, Iran's Ministry of Culture and Islamic Guidance, he had been one of four assistant secretaries to the minister. His work consisted of questioning candidates for the diplomatic service and visiting Iran's embassies to covertly verify whether the ambassador, the employees and their families were trustworthy and answered to Ayatollah Khomeini and Hezbollah. The Argentine delegation then heard that Iran had assembled an intelligence network with members of Hezbollah inside their embassies.

Moatamer had received instructions to fight against Zionism and imperialism, and he attended training camps where he learned to use firearms and explosives. But at some point he turned and ceased to be trustworthy himself: while trying to escape to the United States with his wife and four children, he was abducted by other Iranians in Havana and transported to Caracas so that he could be sent to Tehran. He was lucky – he managed to escape and, a week before the attack in Buenos Aires, he received protection from the United Nations. This is the kind of person you meet thanks to the intelligence services.

"Moatamer said the attack had been planned in Iran and carried out by Hezbollah," Mullen tells me. In fact, on that Saturday when he began his testimony, a movement called Ansar Allah took credit for the attack in a communiqué disseminated in the Lebanese cities of Sidon and Beirut. Apparently it had been revenge for an Israeli operation in Lebanon on 2 June, which had left fifty dead in a Hezbollah encampment. But the organisation did not usually assume direct responsibility for its terrorist attacks, and so the stamp was that of Ansar Allah. For two days, the witness spoke about Iran's network of diplomacy, intelligence and terrorism.

Galeano showed him twenty photos of suspects provided by Mossad. Moatamer said four of them had participated in the 1992 attack on the Israeli embassy. The judge and prosecutors would come to know these unfamiliar names well.

"If they're in Argentina, don't let them leave because there's no doubt they were the ones who took part in the attack," Moatamer continued. Yes – they were or had been in Argentina. Moatamer went on: "The form, the method and the organisation of the attack are decided by members of Hezbollah within the embassy... In all cases, the orders must be received from Iran." And further: "The attacks occurred in Argentina, but they are meant for Israel or the United States."

On 21 March 1994, a few months before the AMIA attack, Moatamer claimed to have attended a large meeting in the home of one of Ayatollah Khamenei's children in Tehran. There, the upcoming attack on the AMIA building was discussed. "Tehran makes a decision and then we know who [inside the embassy] it has been assigned to," he explained. "In turn, those people enlist locals."

> *But why Argentina again, only two years after the Israeli embassy attack?*

The witness seemed trustworthy, and Iran was clearly exporting the Islamist revolution. But why Argentina again, only two years after the Israeli embassy attack? "That is your fault, the weakness is yours," he said. "For them, Argentina is the same as Israel and the United States. The aim is to destroy Israel. Israel has influence here [in Argentina], and since there aren't so many difficulties here, we attack their installations here."

"It was very hard understanding each other," recalls Mullen, the former prosecutor. "The SIDE had brought in an interpreter, but he spoke Arabic, not Farsi, and Moatamer got angry because everything was getting stalled." There were also a few US agents in the room, and one of their interpreters confirmed what the Venezuelan interpreter was saying. The Argentines made a video recording of the testimony and, once back in Buenos Aires, had it translated once again. "What gave it legitimacy was that an attack occurred in London two days later [the bombings of the Israeli embassy and of Balfour House]. Moatamer had mentioned that as well – before it took place."

Just after the delegation returned to Argentina, President Menem met with Judge Galeano at the presidential residence. The secretary of intelligence, Hugo Anzorreguy, had been waiting for the delegation at the airport; he told them that the president was meeting with his cabinet and invited them to come and share their news. It was Monday, 25 July; night.

There was news for them as well: the case had been advancing hour by hour. That afternoon, the Israelis had finally found an engine (right where General Livne had pointed) and, with the discovery of a crater under the rubble, had confirmed the car bomb theory. Tracking down the engine had been important as its serial number might lead to a name.

Scarcely one week had passed and it was clear who would take the leading roles in this story over the coming years: the judge, the alleged local connection and the probable Iranian masterminds. "Alleged", "probable" … time and the lack of resolution force me to use these uncomfortable words.

"Menem said that everything was at the judge's disposal, he could count on whatever [resources] he needed," recalls Mullen. "Moatamer's statement had been recorded on video and was shown, but it was late, around two in the morning, and it was a bit out of control, lots of people were drunk." Menem was known as a good host who knew how to enjoy himself when the sun went down. "Eduardo Bauzá [the chief of the cabinet] was the one who more or less took charge and asked interesting questions," Mullen continues "And the minister of justice was there, [Rodolfo] Barra, who approached me at that moment and said to please respect the secrecy of summary proceedings imposed by the judge, and not talk to anyone."

Judge Galeano believed that Menem was seeking to cut off relations with Iran. Iranian ambassador Hadi Soleimanpour was already under fire – that very afternoon he had gone to the Argentine Chancellery with a letter from the Iranian government in a gesture of peace. Also under fire was his cultural attaché, an enthusiastic Shiite cleric named Mohsen Rabbani, who had visited used car dealerships a few months prior in search of a Renault Trafic (the SIDE had been spying on him since the 1992 attack). But not everyone at the table was prepared to go in that direction. "And who's going to tell Iran that we're cutting off relations?" the chancellor, Guido Di Tella, complained. An official from the chancellery mentioned business relations between Argentina and Iran: US$500 million annually, with a surplus for Argentina. The conversation stretched on and became scattered. Some raised their voices. Others changed the subject. "Let's go," the judge said to his secretary.

Judge Galeano arrived home in the early hours of morning. He was exhausted. The attack had occurred seven days before. *General Livne pointing towards a blanket of rubble, the cadavers in the morgue dotted with metal shrapnel, the SIDE's useless interpreter, Moatamer (could he really be trusted?), tonnes upon tonnes of twisted iron ...* Suddenly Galeano could process no more and fell into a pleasant abyss, only emerging when he awoke the following day.

6.

Wednesday, 27 July 1994. Buenos Aires' Jorge Newbery Airport stood empty that evening. The Plata River lay in repose. A plane crossed the sky. A man who had just returned from Posadas, in Argentina's Misiones Province, was waiting in the arrivals hall, his face marked by doubt. They called him *el Enano* or *el Petiso*, the Dwarf or the Runt. Those who didn't like him called him *el Sapo*, the Toad. His name was Carlos Telleldín.

He liked money, and any business that might prove lucrative: at age eighteen, after a short stint as a trainee in the intelligence services of the Córdoba Province police, he had opened his first used-car shop with the help of his father, a police intelligence chief. In 1994, Telleldín was thirty-three and had managed sexual massage parlours; two nightclubs; a video store; a buy-and-sell shop for antiques, jewellery and gold; a sales network for used appliances; and, once again, a car business. As a result of selling apparently stolen appliances, he had twice faced possible arrest as a suspected accomplice in the robberies. But he had returned from Posadas because he was in an even bigger fix: according to the investigators' initial leads, he had sold the Renault Trafic to the terrorists.

The van had been loaded with 300 kilograms of ammonal – ammonium nitrate and aluminium – a detonator, and soil to direct the blast wave. It is a mixture that can be bought freely. One that leaves behind the unpleasant odour of ammonia.

Telleldín – the Dwarf, the Runt, the Toad: round face, receding hairline, sharp eyes. On 26 July, after the Israelis found the engine from the car bomb, the fence closed in around him and he left the city. Later, he explained that he had done so out of fear that some agents from the Buenos Aires Province police would attack him, perhaps even kill him. According to Telleldín, these agents had extorted him several times, letting him run his business in exchange for money and vehicles. But recently Telleldín had refused and paid less than they were demanding. He was in debt. He said this was the reason he had fled, not the business with the Trafic. What he meant was that he had not collaborated with the terrorists, that he – at least in this matter – was completely innocent.

When agents from the federal police and the SIDE went looking for him at his house in the Villa Ballester suburbs, they found that Telleldín's wife and three children had already let in two Buenos Aires police officers with no apparent connection to the investigation. Talking on the phone with a SIDE agent posted at his house who offered certain guarantees if he would turn himself in, Telleldín decided to return.

Although the SIDE agent had promised that his colleagues would be at the airport, there was no one there. Telleldín called his house from a public telephone: "I'm waiting for you, weren't you going to come get me?" Finally, he was arrested by federal agents.

That night he became the most intriguing suspect in the case – and would remain so for decades. He was accused of being a participant in the attack and knowing about the intended use for the vehicle. He denied it. How much he knew, how much he ignored, how much he was concealing and how much he was cooperating are questions that everyone who investigated him has confronted. But Telleldín – the son of a police intelligence chief – seems to have been cleverer than all of them.

In his initial statements, he recounted that on 8 July – ten days before the attack – he published a notice to sell the van in the newspaper *Clarín*. It was viewed by three Koreans, who arrived in a Mitsubishi Galant and "looked like they came straight out of a poster for some heavy metal band" (according to notes that

Telleldín would later write in prison). The eventual buyer of the Renault Trafic was a man with a Central American accent. He purchased it on 10 July. Of the transaction there remained a bill of sale for 11,500 pesos (then equivalent to US$11,500), with a false document number.

In a famous statement from 5 July 1996, Telleldín changed his story, claiming that the Trafic had actually gone into the hands of the Buenos Aires police officers who were extorting him. This prompted Judge Galeano to arrest the officers and present them as the local connection. What did Telleldín say? That in April 1994 he was arrested and a corrupt police chief named Juan José Ribelli demanded he hand over cash and vehicles in order to recover his freedom and continue in the car sale business. Telleldín handed everything over when he could, but it was not enough. And so, on Sunday, 10 July 1994, a group of police officers came to his home and took the Trafic van as part of the payment towards his debt. These were the two conflicting accounts that Telleldín has given of the Trafic: in one, he sold it to a Central American man; in the other, it was taken by a corrupt police officer.

Telleldín was tried twice and twice acquitted: no one could prove that he knew the buyer or was aware that the Trafic's fate would be the explosion. He convinced nine judges – including three from a higher court that reviewed an appeal against him – yet even so, he remains an enigmatic piece of the puzzle.

In his 2004 book *Caso AMIA: La gran mentira* (*The AMIA Case: The Big Lie*), Telleldín complains that Judge Galeano "came up with a famous line, a hobbyhorse that he used the whole time ... not just him but also the lawsuits and the prosecutors". The line is this: "Telleldín knows more than he's saying."

7.

In prison, where he spent ten years under suspicion of having colluded with the terrorists, Telleldín studied law – which is not uncommon among prisoners in Argentina. By the time he got out he was no longer a businessman but a lawyer. "I started studying because the accusation was so stupid, the four lawyers I took on at the time couldn't explain it to me," he tells me one morning in a small office inside his enormous complex, a three-storey bunker that has a pool but no windows. "I spent years trying to understand that they were accusing me of having staged the result, when in reality I didn't know what the Trafic was going to be used for. I sold four vans: they located three because I sold them just as I said. A guy came in to buy the fourth and he used it for the attack, but I wasn't aware."

Over the years, Telleldín has defended criminals, police officers charged with homicide, and the Chinese mafia, and has worked on more than 200 drug-trafficking cases, including at least one with Los Monos, the most harmful drug ring in the country. Things have gone well for him. Now he is something of a magnate – he owns two Mercedes-Benzes and makes, at a minimum, "two judges' salaries" per month – US$20,000 or more (perhaps a slight modesty leads him to obscure the exact figure). He has won acquittals that seemed impossible. He has opened branches of his practice in multiple cities. He has made large real estate deals. And he has taken advantage of his controversial past; in 2022, he tweeted: "Telleldín & Associates Law Firm – our goal is to be the best legal practice in criminal matters, we know criminal affairs. Acquitted twice AMIA case."

"I can tell you two things about the AMIA case," he says. "That it screwed up my life because they kept me imprisoned illegally for ten years. And that as a result I made a petition to the state in the Inter-American Commission on Human Rights because a person can be processed for two years at maximum, but it's been twenty-eight for me already." Telleldín's revenge could cost Argentina US$7 million.

He says that what interests him now is not money but rather a legal victory against Argentina, which would completely vindicate him and reinstate his rights. That would allow him to travel freely around the world and visit the daughter who lives in Orlando, Florida. At one point we hear the noise of children who have just returned from primary school – these are his younger children. Their faces appear in framed photos, and they look like him. He has eleven kids in total, aged between one and forty-two.

"The guy who bought the Trafic said his name was Ramón Martínez," he continues, "and it's more than proved that he used false identification. A terrorist isn't going to show up with his real name. At that time I was a businessman, I was selling, I didn't have the authority to say 'Show me your papers'."

In 1994, Telleldín was selling around ten vehicles per month. But that Trafic was special: it was a *twin*. The matter is difficult to follow and begins with a previous Trafic van that was burned in a fire. The remains of the burnt van were bought by a business owned by Alejandro Monjo that sold used and junk vehicles. But the van's documentation remained valid because the fire was never reported.

Monjo sold that Trafic and its documentation to Telleldín. And Telleldín delegated a task to two mechanics: extract its engine and install it inside another Trafic, one a thief had just stolen. In the end, the second van was ready to go with the engine and documentation from the first. Telleldín then sold it as a used vehicle with legal documentation, when in reality it was a stolen Trafic – that is to say, a *twin*. (He admitted as much in his 2004 book.) This was the van in the explosion. The number of the original engine was the end of the ball of yarn that led back to Telleldín.

Like any good lawyer, Telleldín knows that words create the world. Like any good car salesman, he knows that everything is negotiable. He swears that he's telling the whole truth and considers himself a scapegoat in the case.

The file on the case is full of differing versions, revisions and myths. Telleldín relates how he lived in an apartment on Calle Roosevelt for a while, across from a synagogue. People said that he used to throw antisemitic pamphlets from his window. "Nothing like that," he tells me. "I'd get in line at the synagogue when they brought clothes [charity handouts] from Europe – have you seen what they give the Jews? I'd take Armani, Givenchy, I'd take a few suits ... Later they said I threw out pamphlets. I'd never think of a pamphlet, if they gave me clothing!" He relates this without laughing, almost bitter. Words, stories and names flow through him like a river.

> *"Telleldín is a very intelligent person, but he is 100 per cent devoted to crime"*

"Telleldín is a very intelligent person," the former prosecutor Mullen had told me. "But he is 100 per cent devoted to crime. I think he knew how to manipulate all the information he had, and he's been very dishonest."

"Car salesmen always get a bad rap," Telleldín says in his defence.

8.

Jacobo Chemanuel, the maintenance worker who had been rescued from under seven metres of rubble after thirty-one hours, died near the end of that first week, on Friday, 22 July 1994. The crushing force he had endured had destroyed his circulation and kidney function.

Augusto Daniel Jesús, a boy of nineteen, died in the attack along with his mother, María Lourdes Jesús, who had been taking an aged care class at the AMIA. Augusto had been accompanying her. For many years Augusto could not be identified; only a piece of bone and another piece of muscle were left to match with someone's DNA one day in the future. Often the investigators saw in such remains the phantom face of the suicidal driver, whom they were trying to identify among all the human remains left by the explosion, though without success. In 2016 it was finally confirmed that the bone and muscle fragments belonged to Augusto Daniel Jesús.

Naúm Javier Tenenbaum, a lawyer, had gone to the AMIA to organise the shloshim ceremony for his father, who had died a month before. His daughter, the writer Tamara Tenenbaum, wrote: "There are things/ that to be made into/ poems/ need only be told. / My father died/ on the day/ he went to AMIA/ to do the paperwork/ for burying his father/ (my grandfather)/ in the cemetery/ of La Tablada./ Done."

The AMIA building was undergoing some renovations that day. Andrés Malamud, the architect in charge, was carrying $6000 in his pocket to pay the construction workers, but when his body turned up among the debris someone stole the money. He was athletic, obsessive, a family man. His widow, Diana Wassner, smiles wistfully, remembering him. When I ask what he was like, the first thing she says is: "He was young."

On Thursday, 21 July (three days after the attack), a rally of 150,000 people gathered in light rain opposite the National Congress to condemn terrorism. There were a few banners and some photos of people still missing. The silence of their pain was interrupted by occasional whistles and boos from under the umbrellas, aimed at the political authorities. Menem opted not to speak.

From those earliest days, the president was blamed for the state's indifference to preventing this second terrorist attack. Menem began to be seen as an accomplice by act or omission. "At no point did he even show signs of helping uncover the truth for the victims' relatives and for society," reads one tweet from Memoria Activa – the main group of relatives of victims – published after his death in 2021.

> "In what way did the government benefit by covering up a crime like that? Quite the contrary"

Menem was tried for concealment (the suspicion was that he had prevented some leads from being investigated), but he was acquitted in 2019. "And so Menem died as he lived: unpunished," concludes the tweet.

"We're asking them to follow up on all the leads that weren't followed," Wassner, the leader of Memoria Activa as well as the architect's widow, tells me during her lunch break. "It doesn't matter which lead: just for it to be investigated. For the state to do what it needs to do. For it to at least be known what happened, because just thinking about justice in the AMIA case ... it's hard. For it to be known who committed the attack, why they committed it, how they committed it."

A year and a half after the former president's death, Carlos Vladimiro Corach, one of his most active ministers, explains to me that in 1994 such things had never occurred in Argentina and no one had any experience in dealing with terrorists: not the government, not the opposition party, not the security forces, not the judges. However, this is not entirely true. Argentina had already known one similar case: the attack on the Israeli embassy, committed in 1992, possibly by the same people.

Corach was named minister of the interior – and therefore chief of police – on 5 January 1995, six months after the attack. In those days he never left the president's side. He was a shrewd man, Jewish, a lawyer, an operator in high politics and a Perónist, though there were rumours he was named after Karl Marx and Vladimir Lenin. (His mother told him she had given him these names because she enjoyed Russian literature.) Now eighty-seven years old, Corach has lost none of the cleverness in his eyes, which dart around constantly.

"For the government, the AMIA case was a fundamental issue," he tells me. "And for the president it was a very hard blow. Because the president had ties to the Jewish community." As a baby, Menem had had a Jewish wet nurse, Corach says. And he was the first Argentine president to visit Israel. "I went with him. There was a marvellous reception." In a hallway of his office, caricatures of Corach from opposition newspapers in the 1990s appear in frames. Sometimes the former minister amuses himself by reading them.

"The idea that we wanted to cover it up is nonsense," Corach says emphatically, suddenly energetic. "In what way did the government benefit by covering up a crime like that? Quite the contrary. Our government had the best relationship with the State of Israel." Then, as if all these suspicions were childish fables, he ends in a friendly tone. "Nothing would have been a greater benefit and triumph for the government than to discover something about that matter. It would have meant glory."

9.

What exactly was President Menem accused of covering up? I'm not sure if many people really know. In general terms, he was suspected of impeding the progress of a different trail from that of the Iranian diplomats: the Syria lead, which we will also call the dumpster lead here. This trail had a protagonist named Alberto Jacinto Kanoore Edul, a textile impresario – the kind who travelled around with a chauffeur and, in that era, had a cellular phone installed in his Peugeot 505, the kind whose father was an old friend of the president's. (Both families were originally from the Syrian town of Yabroud, also the birthplace of the notorious arms trafficker Monzer al-Kassar, who obtained an Argentine passport during Menem's government.) Kanoore Edul senior would enter the Government House without having to pass through security, and used to visit officials in the embassies of Lebanon, Syria and Morocco, possibly in his role as treasurer of the Argentine–Arab Chamber of Commerce.

Three things place Kanoore Edul's son at the centre of the case. One: at 3.30 p.m. on Sunday, 10 July 1994, eight days before the attack, he called Carlos Telleldín from his cell phone. The Trafic had just been delivered to the man that Telleldín identified as Ramón Martínez. Kanoore Edul junior stated that he did not remember that call and attributed it to his chauffeur, but he did admit he had been looking for a van because his own, a Mercedes-Benz, had recently been stolen. Two: contact information appeared in his appointment book for eleven mechanics workshops as well as the phone number of Mohsen Rabbani, the cultural attaché of the Iranian embassy, who was a suspect in those early days and who had searched for a used Trafic before the attack. Three: a truck from a company called Santa Rita – owned by a Lebanese man,

Nassib Haddad – left a dumpster for rubble collection outside the door of the AMIA just before the attack, and another dumpster in an empty lot under a highway in Constitución 2657, in the San Cristóbal neighbourhood, next to one of Kanoore Edul's properties.

Judge Galeano tapped three of Kanoore Edul's phone lines, and on 1 August 1994 ordered three raids. But on the morning of that same day, one of the federal police commissioners heading the raids, Jorge "Fino" Palacios, strangely communicated with Kanoore Edul senior, who in turn met with Menem that afternoon. (He most likely went in person, but it is also possible that another family member went in his place.) Two raids were performed even as the meeting was occurring, during which, according to prosecutor Alberto Nisman's 2009 hypothesis, the president told his brother (a Government House official) to reprimand the judge – and therefore undermine the Syria lead. There was no third raid, the phone taps stopped and the transcripts that had been presented disappeared. Kanoore Edul junior was later arrested but stated nothing of interest: he was like shredded paper. (In 2009, a federal judge prosecuted Menem's brother for the crime of cover-up, but he died the following year.)

A tribunal acquitted Menem of shutting down the Syria lead, and Galeano denies having been pressured. Kanoore Edul senior died in 2010, and the shadow over Kanoore Edul junior lingered until September 2021, when the public prosecutor's office asked that he be dismissed from the case, along with twelve others accused within the framework of the Syria lead.

The dumpster is the maddening piece in this part of the puzzle. The version involving the Trafic has been debated several times, but it never changed. "The official story of the car bomb allows no doubt," gripes Horacio Lutzky, a lawyer and journalist and the author of an investigative book about the AMIA attack. "They [the leadership of AMIA and DAIA] elevated it to the category of religious truth: if you debate it, they very nearly accuse you of antisemitism."

There are several messy details surrounding the Trafic. The record of the discovery of its engine, for example, was signed by a firefighter as the witness, but this man later stated that he never saw the engine. Or another: there are only two people who witnessed the Trafic driving towards its target, and they are not very reliable. Lutzky is inclined to believe that there were two explosions: the first inside the dumpster, which set off another inside the building. The elevator operator stated strange bags – explosives? – had been brought in amid the confusion of the renovations. "These are striking things that go against the official story," Lutzky tells me.

> "If someone talks to you with certainty about the attack they're talking nonsense"

The future president Cristina Fernández de Kirchner – back then a high-profile legislator who supported Memoria Activa, the main group of victims' relatives – did not believe the official story either. In a meeting of the committee created by congress to oversee the investigation, she admonished Judge Galeano. "You don't want to follow the dumpster lead," she said again and again.

The dumpster was the property of a business devoted to mining and the transport of rubble. The business was named after Santa Rita, patron saint of impossible causes. Nassib Haddad, the owner, is a most unusual character. Born in Aynata, Lebanon, he was rumoured to be the cousin of Ayatollah Muhammad Husayn Fadlallah, one of the founders of Hezbollah and a declared enemy of Israel. (However, there is a report in the case's judiciary file in which the SIDE advises that there is no proof of this family connection.)

As part of his work in mining, he bought explosives, fuses and detonators. In October 1993, he acquired ammonium nitrate from the Delbene y Serris factory in Olvarría, a rural agro-industrial city. Given the investigators believed the AMIA explosion was caused by ammonium nitrate, Nassib Haddad was detained for a few hours at the beginning of August 1994.

"It makes no sense to take a dumpster to [an empty lot], unless you consider that it was selected for disarming the bomb in the event that it could not be placed in the AMIA," said Gabriel Levinas, a journalist who headed a DAIA investigative team and published his questions in the book *La ley bajo los escombros* (*Law Under the Rubble*). At the same time, it is reported in the legal file that a dumpster had been hired for a clean-up at the lot. Levinas is either unaware of this or does not believe it. "I'm not in the least bit certain about what it is that happened, and if someone talks to you with certainty about the attack they're talking nonsense," he warns me.

Andrés Malamud, the architect in charge of the AMIA renovations, was the one who called for the dumpster. His studio had been working with Santa Rita for some time. But the delivery receipt, which shows Malamud receiving the dumpster, has a fake signature.

The case is a mosaic of doubt. But in the end, one of the most important questions is this: why would President Menem want to eliminate a lead? Surely not to save his friend Kanoore Edul, who, in fact, ended up estranged from him. There are other motives. Several of them.

"Menem turned 180 degrees when he came into power," Horacio Lutzky tells me. His book is a geopolitical analysis revealing that in 1988, a year before winning his first presidential election, Menem received more than US$40 million in support from the Middle East. He had promised Syria the same nuclear technology that Argentina had already pledged to sell to Iran. There had been Argentine engineers in Tehran, and in December 1991 a ship loaded with nuclear material had been due to set out for Iran. To attract more allies, Menem then travelled to Syria and held a meeting with President Hafez al-Assad. (Arms trafficker Monzer al-Kassar acted as interpreter, according to an investigation by *Río Negro*.)

> *So it was that the candidate Menem financed his political dream*

He also told Libya that he could offer them the Condor II missile, an Argentine medium-range missile for unconventional loads, financed by a German company and with one sure buyer: Iraq. Colonel Muammar Gaddafi was already aware of the Argentine missile project because he had visited Buenos Aires in the 1970s and met with then president Juan Domingo Perón. Gaddafi gave Menem $10 million, according to Nemen Nader Rodríguez, a Dominican businessman who acted as a go-between (as reported by Lutzky).

So it was that the candidate Menem financed his political dream.

"But when he takes over, he cancels all those plans," Lutzky continues. The United States was aware of his promises to the Arabs and forced an end to everything in a meeting between Argentine chancellor Domingo Cavallo and US secretary of state James Baker. At that time, Menem and Gaddafi saw each other at the Libyan embassy in Belgrade, at a forum for the Non-Aligned

Movement. The embassy had palm trees, camels and dates. Gaddafi was guarded by an armed woman. When Menem mentioned that he was receiving US support, the colonel was irritated. "You can only gain an advantage over the Americans if you have military power," he told him. "That's why I showed so much interest in the Condor missile." Cavallo witnessed this and recounted it in his book *El peso de la verdad* (*The Weight of the Truth*).

"Menem becomes a close ally of the United States," Lutzky continues, "and he uses the Jewish community as a golden bridge. He visits Israel in October 1991 and, on top of that, sends two ships to the Persian Gulf War. There was a whole sum of episodes experienced as betrayal. And all of this, when it comes to evaluating where Hezbollah might carry out its vengeance, gives more than one meaning to Argentina."

The president was never going to admit to his unfulfilled promises. But the interested parties would hardly forget them.

10.

Now we must go back to the first days of 1993.

In a room of the Hotel Marta in Zurich, something very strange occurred. This story was told in a statement to the Argentine federal police by a Brazilian named Wilson Dos Santos, a man of doubtful virtues who was missing a finger – or possibly an entire hand. (I say "doubtful" because, according to one of his friends, Dos Santos was quick to make deals and plot schemes.) In Buenos Aires, where he travelled to buy and sell clothing, Dos Santos had met an Iranian woman in April 1992. Isabella. He had seen her in a café: dark hair down to her waist, bright eyes. He talked to her. She responded. They hit it off and exchanged phone numbers. They started going out.

They almost always ended up in a hotel. Isabella lived in a boarding house with other young women; Dos Santos quickly understood that she charged for sex, though that was not the case with him.

Leaving behind a life under the Islamist regime, Isabella had arrived in Buenos Aires five years before, a place where it was easy to get residency and a jumping-off point to get to Canada, the country she wanted to live in. Dos Santos started getting to know her world: Iranian friends scattered around the city, nights drinking in bars, a congressman who paid. In November 1992, things were going well and they decided they could try their luck in Europe and apply for a Canadian visa there. Isabella bought tickets to Zurich at a travel agency and when they picked them up, Dos Santos saw her real name on her passport: Nasrin Mokhtari.

From Switzerland they went to Italy. There they tried for the visa, but the application was denied because her identification seemed false. They returned to Zurich, barely speaking. Mokhtari was quite upset. Things between them cooled.

They were staying at the Hotel Marta, in the city centre. They took separate rooms. That night, Dos Santos saw Mokhtari from a distance, in a hallway, dressed in a traditional black tunic. The next morning at breakfast, Dos Santos discovered Alí Slim, one of Mokhtari's Iranian friends from Buenos Aires, at a table in the dining room. With her. Dos Santos hid, and after the man left Dos Santos followed Mokhtari up to her room and asked her what all this was about. Mokhtari said she would explain it to him later. They had breakfast downstairs and then she invited him back up to her room.

Inside there were two aluminium suitcases.

She smiled, he asked if she had gone shopping, she pushed him down onto the bed. They had sex. When Mokhtari got up, she opened one of the suitcases. And then he saw the money. Bills upon bills. Thousands of dollars. He did a mental calculation and believed three million would not be an exaggeration. Suddenly Mokhtari's smile trembled, she turned serious, started to speak, and the first tears appeared. She spoke to him about her life; she showed him photos of herself in military uniform holding a machine gun; she took out three passports, one from Iran, another from Lebanon, and the one from Argentina; she confessed that, along with Alí Slim, she had taken part in the attack on the Israeli embassy in Buenos Aires in 1992; and she said that she had to go back for another job, but not until July of the following year, 1994. It was an intense, hours-long conversation. In the end she asked him not to abandon her, said that they could live together anywhere. Except Iran or Argentina.

Suddenly Alí Slim entered the room. Without explaining the strangeness of his presence in Switzerland, he invited them to dinner. It was almost night now. At the table, Slim studied Dos Santos and, over the following days, asked him to help fill more suitcases in Rome and Munich. Dos Santos, terrified, fled.

A year passed. At the beginning of July 1994, we find him in Turin, looking for work alongside Sandra, his new girlfriend. One day he tells her everything: Isabella, the suitcases, the machine gun, the Iranian man, the unresolved matter in Buenos Aires. And Sandra convinces him that he needs to let the authorities know. Dos Santos presents himself at the Brazilian consulate. There, they tell him he needs to talk to the Israelis. He does so. After his statement they say they're going to call back, but they never do. Then he goes to the Argentine consulate. Little or nothing happens there: why would they believe him?

A few days later, the AMIA explodes.

11.

The story of Nasrin Mokhtari and Wilson Dos Santos is contained in a binder inside the AMIA file. The binders are separate sections addressing various theories. There were so many leads and so much to investigate that the file became a labyrinth. Or worse: "A black hole … that swallows everything and destroys as it goes," writes Miguel Bronfman, the AMIA's lead lawyer, in a book over 800 pages long. Today there are 422 binders, containing up to 354,000 pages. In 2022, seventeen binders remained unresolved.

The binder on Mokhtari and Dos Santos ran until 2007. The adventure ended with a conviction for false testimony during criminal proceedings for him and a dismissal for her. In November 1994, Dos Santos stated that he had lied to get money from anyone who wanted to buy an exclusive. It seems that Alí Slim never existed. Nor the suitcases filled with cash. However, Dos Santos' tour around Europe with Mokhtari and his explosive warnings at the consulates – days before the bombing – really happened.

Mokhtari was detained and investigated for years over the two terrorist attacks. She spoke several times to journalists waiting outside the courthouse doors, claiming she had been raped by the police officers who guarded her inside the court. But her accusations never received justice. Alone in a hostile country, denied permission to leave it, she deteriorated rapidly. In 2005, a legal ruling that dismissed a complaint she had made to Judge Galeano described her as "lacking in cohesion or coherence". She sold her body, begged, did stints in the Moyano neuropsychiatric hospital. I tried to find her in the city. She is a spectre, about whom no one knows anything.

As for the binders, which had emerged as a solution to the chaos, Memoria Activa denounced them as a strategy by the judge to conceal his letters. Very quickly, the AMIA case began to leave

Galeano in an ambiguous position. To investigate the attack was to investigate corruption. The case was a plague, and Galeano became infected. Both Memoria Activa, trying to uncover the truth, and the defence lawyers, trying to defend their clients' rights, accused him of going outside the law to obtain information from the accused, of intercepting lawyers' phone calls, of pressuring detainees. Of so much more. But the Jewish leadership backed him, and the political powers did as well. For a while.

In his first ruling, the Judge Galeano indicated that the attack had been committed with a Renault Trafic, using ammonal as the explosive agent. He described how Hezbollah organised its attacks abroad and mentioned the cleric Mohsen Rabbani. He charged Carlos Telleldín with concealing evidence and called for the international arrest of the Iranian men identified by Manuchehr Moatamer. It was 9 August 1994: not yet one month since the attack and the case appeared to be solved.

But, as we know, things became complicated. And in 1996 the judge made a mistake in his strategy.

"Galeano may have made blunders, but he's someone who gave up his life for this investigation," the former prosecutor Mullen told me. "What he produced in the investigation is enormous. Then the tree overshadowed the forest: one error overshadowed a serious investigation … He considered what he'd done to be legal, but the justice system did not. If it had been legal, we wouldn't have gotten dragged into it."

12.

With Telleldín in prison, Judge Galeano had believed he would get a confession out of him. On 30 July 1994, Telleldín gave his first statement, in which he mentioned the Koreans and the Central American. On 6 August, he added that there were some Buenos Aires Province cops who wanted him to hand over 40,000 pesos or else be locked up in a cell. He also gave statements on 7 August, 29 December and 4 April 1995. Every time he spoke, he remembered more. He invented and misled, in the opinion of those who distrusted him.

In August 1995, he received a visit – from Luisa Riva Aramayo, the president of the National Court of Appeals in Criminal Affairs and Federal Corrections, who was allegedly under orders from Minister Corach. A woman with a Thatcherian spirit, she returned several times, trying to make Telleldín give up information. Riva Aramayo asked him to write a book containing everything about the extortion he had suffered at the hands of the police. On her fourth visit – as Telleldín relates in the book he ultimately did publish – Riva Aramayo said she was bringing word from Menem and Corach: "We don't want any more car thieves, we don't want any more garnish." She ordered him to declare that the police had taken the van. If he didn't, he would be sentenced as a willing participant in the attack. In their next meeting, Telleldín admitted that he was cornered. He would do what they asked.

So it was that the informal meetings with Judge Galeano began – encounters captured by a hidden camera installed by the SIDE – in which they discussed Telleldín's upcoming statement, as well as the money he would receive in exchange.

This is the judge's account: Telleldín spoke of that police chief named Juan José Ribelli, who was the head of the Investigations Brigade in Lanús, a team of detectives viewed as a gang of outlaws. That was the golden age of the police mafia. According to Galeano, Telleldín and his crew were protected by Ribelli, and they would give him a cut in exchange for staying in the business of selling stolen cars. The Renault Trafic that exploded at the AMIA was part of one of those payments Telleldín made to Ribelli. The next question that interested the judge was what Ribelli had done with the van, and whether he had sold it to the terrorists at the end of the line.

"I need 400,000 dollars," the prisoner Telleldín demanded, according to Galeano. "I don't want my freedom, I want that money to protect my family."

"For the first time, Telleldín was holding before me the price of the truth he knew," Galeano later said. He believed that buying this information was acceptable. After all, surely that is the reason there was – and still is – a reward fund. Telleldín did not want to make a statement against the police because, who knows? Maybe one day his whole family would turn up dead. Telleldín had already spent two years in prison, and Galeano believed he was still covering for the people who had taken the van. He needed Telleldín to make a statement on the record. Galeano communicated with the secretary of intelligence, Anzorreguy, who was in agreement about paying Telleldín.

On 1 July 1996, Galeano received Telleldín in the courthouse. They discussed the payment and the statement. Telleldín told the judge that his partner, Ana Boragni, and his lawyer, Víctor Stinfale, would take care of receiving the money. (I contacted Boragni – who is no longer Telleldín's partner – for an interview. She told me she did not want to relive any of that history.) Galeano once again asked Telleldín about a few things that would appear in his statement. The judge followed a roster of questions drafted by the SIDE, which had an agent in another office watching the video live.

Galeano decided to use the hidden camera because they were discussing someone else's money, in case he needed to assess the advisability of the payment, and because he would need to remember what was said. Also to cover his back. Galeano did not seem to fear that the video might fall into someone else's hands and go off like a bomb. Once it was recorded, Galeano would keep the cassette in the safe of one of his secretaries – a safe that contained VHS tapes of other filmed statements, which the team at the court used for their work, watching them over and over. Often, while that was occurring, the safe would be left open.

Here is Telleldín's account, as he told it to me: "For the payment I told him [the judge]: 'I want a million.' 'No, there's 400,000' ... we fought it out like the sale of a car. The deal was that I'd get my freedom in '97, I'd be cut out of all that and be left in peace. In exchange, I had to state that the van was taken by Ribelli, which wasn't the case."

I tried to interview Ribelli. He said he was away travelling. I asked if we could talk on his return. "We'll see," he said, and never responded again.

> "That was my strategy from prison: to show that the whole investigation was a fraud"

Telleldín signed his new statement on 5 July, after a phone call in which his partner confirmed that the payment had been made. (With the money, she bought a newsstand in the Vicente López neighbourhood, near where they lived.) In his statement, Telleldín went over the brigades' extortions and said that at 2.30 p.m. on 10 July 1994 a person showed up at his home disguised in a wig, glasses and a cap. A police officer. He was there for the Trafic.

Those words put Ribelli and three other agents in prison. Now it was expected that they would reveal to whom they had given the van. But five years later, at the beginning of the trial, Telleldín revealed that his statement had been a lie. "That was my strategy from prison: to show that the whole investigation was a fraud," he told me.

There is more: in March 1997, someone stole the VHS tape of the meeting between Galeano and Telleldín from a safe in the courthouse. That video made its way to Ribelli. While imprisoned, Ribelli requested a meeting with Galeano. A few days later, he sat before the judge, took a VHS from an envelope, and slid it across the desk. He said: "This came to me, and it's too hot for me to handle. Watch it on your own, without your children." (Telleldín relates this in his book. Ribelli denies having said those words, but does admit to having received the video and slid it across the judge's desk.)

The footage was aired on the TV programme *Día D* with the journalist Jorge Lanata, and the scandal of seeing the judge and the suspect talking about money set off an avalanche.

Somehow, Galeano survived.

13.

Let's stay a bit longer in 1997 – the year the footage of Galeano and Telleldín was broadcast on television and a scandal shook up the case.

That same year it was made public that sixty-six audio cassettes had gone missing, tapes that contained recordings of tapped phone calls – of Telleldín, of the Iranians implicated, of spies engaged in strange activities. The cassettes had gone missing from both Section 85 (SIDE counterintelligence) and DPOC (the Department for Protection of the Constitutional Order, the federal police division pursuing the case). This meant that someone with a great deal of power wanted to cover something up. Section 85 and the DPOC were not even allied forces: they mistrusted each other and were in competition.

"Too much of a coincidence," says Claudio Lifschitz, the former vice-secretary of Galeano's court who exposed several blunders in the investigation. Lifschitz had come to the court in 1995, newly arrived from the federal police: he was an official in the police intelligence services and a lawyer. One police chief, Palacios, had recommended him to Judge Galeano to audit the SIDE's activities in the case. "I don't trust anyone and whatever I have to investigate, even if it was my poor mother, may she rest in peace, I'd investigate her too," Lifschitz tells me. We're talking over the phone: he lives in Alicante, Spain, where he works as a lawyer. He left Argentina in 2019 after receiving a threat at his home. Before that he had been attacked twice in the street and had the word "AMIA" carved into his back with a knife.

Lifschitz discovered – and revealed – that the file was full of holes. Memoria Activa and Cristina Fernández de Kirchner respect him for this reason. But Galeano and Mullen are convinced he was the one who stole the VHS tape of the Galeano–Telleldín meeting.

His explorations led him to examine records held by the federal court in Lomas de Zamora, which held jurisdiction over the Ezeiza international airport. There, the SIDE had investigated an alleged Iranian terrorist cell – something almost no one knew, and the significance of which would reveal the ambiguous role that the intelligence agency played in the case. This story begins on 4 April 1994, three months before the AMIA attack, when an Iranian man, Khalil Ghatea, tried to get onto a plane with a stolen English passport. He was arrested, and the local head judge, Patricio Santa Marina, took on the case. On 11 July, one week before the attack,

Ghatea requested permission to travel and obtained it. However, when he went to the airport a week after the attack, on 25 July, authorities were not allowing Iranians to leave the country. The Court of Appeals referred the case to Galeano.

On the day of the attack, 18 July, Judge Santa Marina and the SIDE tapped the phones of a few Iranians of interest and … surprise: the cleric Mohsen Rabbani communicated with Ghatea. What did they discuss? We do not know. But the important thing is: Judge Santa Marina and the SIDE clearly had information on Rabbani and some other Iranians prior to the attack.

Santa Marina complied with the order from the Court of Appeals and sent Ghatea's file to Galeano. But then Judge Santa Marina invented another case (using the pretext of an anonymous call warning of an attack against President Menem) and, working with the SIDE, tapped the same phone lines again. He created a *twin case* so as not to leave the spies out of the plot.

"It's architecture for a cover-up," Lifschitz tell me. "The Secretariat of Intelligence knew about the [AMIA] attack and did not prevent it. They have the truth of the story, they've been listening to the phones for months. Why weren't those wiretaps [of Ghatea's case] turned over to the [AMIA] case?" He refers to the sixty-six missing audio cassettes.

Lifschitz's theory, which he published in a book as a kind of insurance in case something happened to him, is that the SIDE had a mole inside the Iranian cell, who was spying on it for months. But the SIDE let the Iranian cell go at the last minute because of some political order or because the van escaped the mole's notice. And so the attack occurred. "And no way will the Secretariat of Intelligence or the presidency ever take responsibility and tell you they were involved or facilitated it, for whatever reason, whether because of a poorly made political decision or because they withdrew out of negligence."

Maybe the answers were contained in those sixty-six missing audio cassettes.

14.

Three years went by. On some days the picture of the investigation appeared to be coming along, and on other days it was shadowed by the brushstrokes of the Syria lead, by the dark disguises and trickery of the SIDE spies. During the memorial event on 18 July 1997, Laura Ginsberg, from Memoria Activa, said: "I accuse the government of condoning injustice." Minister Corach stood there, unmoved, the target of jeers. In the afternoon, Rubén Beraja of the DAIA said that he regretted the expressions of grievance and that there were differences between the institution's position and that of "Señora Ginsberg".

That year, the cleric Mohsen Rabbani went back to Iran, Argentina compensated Iran for the cancellation of the nuclear contracts, and Galeano travelled to Paris to meet with the MKO, an Iranian opposition organisation that was giving him more names to investigate.

Also in that year, finally, the prosecutor Mullen – who worked alongside another prosecutor, José Barbaccia – began preparing to bring the case to trial. The prosecutors could see the horizon and thought that bringing on a third prosecutor would help. They met with their chief and told him they needed someone dynamic and capable, someone prepared to analyse an infinite file.

Mullen suggested a candidate: a federal trial prosecutor from the San Martín Department. A young man with a good background and a fantastic memory, and a certain reputation for being ambitious and showy, who wanted to leave behind the case he was then working on, which dealt with a bloody attack on a military base by a Guevarist commando. "I shared a table with him at the wedding of one of my employees, and I explained it, I told him what we were dealing with," recalls Mullen. It was not a chat lost between glasses of champagne. He was offering the man a place on the prosecution team for the biggest case in Argentine history. "He was hooked, his eyes shone and he turned red."

The third prosecutor's name was Alberto Nisman.

15.

The trial began in September 2001. The explosion had occurred seven years earlier; the passage of time was infuriating for the victims' families, for the nation. Telleldín, Ribelli and three of the latter's subordinates were being tried, along with fifteen others – former police and civilians – for crimes indirectly related to the attack: unlawful association, false imprisonment, extortion, automobile theft and so on. The trial had more than 1200 witnesses.

The prosecutor's case was based on the existence of an agreement between the police and Telleldín, who the prosecutors did not doubt was a professional criminal. But little by little the trial started to take another course, and neither the prosecutors nor the plaintiffs – except perhaps those from Memoria Activa – felt very comfortable. "At times," wrote Bronfman, the AMIA's lawyer, "one had a feeling that the very collapse of the building had to be proved, as it seemed that even that fact was called into doubt."

With every passing day the three judges in the tribunal were more troubled by the investigation that had been conducted in the court of Galeano. All of Galeano's employees were called to testify. And when it was proved that Telleldín had received the payment of $400,000, the trial over the local connection became the trial over the investigating judge.

The ending was stunning. The tribunal declared that everything the court had done since the police entered the scene with Telleldín's statement regarding Ribelli in October 1995 was corrupt. After determining that the payment received by Telleldín was illegal, the tribunal designated everything that followed – such as the charge against the police officers – as unlawful. And that

> *The accused in the case were acquitted and Galeano was thrown to the wolves*

extended backwards as well. Almost everything was "void". One of the few things left standing was the theory of the car bomb. The secret payment made with SIDE money was poisoning everything: the tribunal considered that Telleldín had been paid to lie. His strategy – "to show that the whole investigation was a fraud" – was bearing fruit.

Before the beginning of the trial, the prosecutor Nisman had told Mullen he was sure they would succeed in the sentencing of the police officers. But when he was supposed to appeal, he did not do so. Nor did he respond when the tribunal, at Telleldín's request, removed Mullen and Barbaccia. (On the contrary, he requested sick leave and stopped answering Mullen's calls.)

"Nisman betrayed us," Mullen told me. Mullen left the courtroom downcast and defeated, realising everything was over.

The sentence was 4819 pages long. The accused in the case were acquitted and Galeano was thrown to the wolves.

A press release from the court says: "It was possible to establish, due to numerous confirmed irregularities, that the investigating judge directed his actions towards 'constructing' an incriminating theory, thereby pretending to meet the logical demands of society while at the same time satisfying the dark interests of unscrupulous leaders." The tribunal filed criminal complaints against former president Menem, the judge, the prosecutors and some other officials. It was 2004. A decade had already passed. The next year, Galeano was dismissed.

16.

Juan José Galeano sits before me in his office, adjusting his clip-on glasses. In the 1990s he was an Eliot Ness, a mud-spattered untouchable. He has traded in his scratchy suits for Ralph Lauren shirts in a modern cut, dedicated himself to a passion for jazz (one day he is listening to the pianist Adrián Iaies when he receives me) and, unexpectedly, become a hatha yoga instructor.

In his office, a bright room with high ceilings and wooden floors, there is a black zafu, a blue pyramid, a compass and a few bowls. A wooden Buddha rests on the bookcase alongside heavy legal tomes. And there are two saxophones, dozens of CDs and an audio setup. The day before this interview, Galeano guided a meditation session over Zoom. He tried yoga for the first time in 2005, after he was dismissed: "I needed to slow down my thoughts and my RPMs," he explains.

"At that time, and also at present, there was an active reward for $2 million (now $3 million) for any information that could be provided about the attack," he tells me. Unsurprisingly, he has never been able to distance himself from the AMIA case. It is etched into his retinas, revealed in the creases that appear in his broad forehead when he raises his eyebrows. He speaks of it in serene tones, like a prayer. Word by word, the old judge tells of his rise and fall.

"Telleldín was asking for money," he continues, "and it seemed appropriate to me to have a record of that situation, where he was asking for part of the fund that the state would give in exchange for the information he claimed to have." His information was crucial: what Telleldín said might lead the investigators to the terrorists. "We thought the best way would be to record it, to ask him questions to see what it was that he could provide." It was "a legal situation [that involved] a secret operation", he said in an interview with *La Nación* in July 2015, a month before the second trial, over concealed evidence, began.

This trial, sparked by the indictments of the 2004 tribunal, was truly major. At issue were the payment to Telleldín, the complaint against the Buenos Aires police and the concealment of the Syria lead. In addition to Galeano, the defendants included former president Menem, former prosecutors Mullen and Barbaccia, former intelligence secretary Anzorreguy, former intelligence undersecretary Juan Carlos Anchézar, former DAIA president Beraja, former commissioners Jorge Palacios and Carlos Castañeda, Telleldín, his former partner Ana Boragni, his old lawyer Víctor Stinfale, and one more SIDE agent. Ten federal judges recused themselves from serving in the tribunal.

Finally, in 2019, the hammer fell: Mullen, Barbaccia, Anzorreguy, Anchézar, Castañeda and Boragni were sentenced. As were Telleldín, to three and a half years in prison (which would likely be covered by the time he had already served), and Galeano, to six years.

The convictions are not yet settled. Galeano remains at liberty, as does Telleldín. The appeal submitted by Galeano is 1054 pages long; it is unknown when the higher court will rule.

Since 2015, the former judge has given no interviews. Now he is recounting his story once again. "I may have made mistakes, there may have been errors, but in no way did I commit a crime," he tells me. Our two conversations are long – now and then he takes a page from his files, or prints out the text of some law – but he asks me not to record much. His downfall began earlier, he says, when he investigated President Néstor Kirchner (who was in office from 2003 to 2007) in a case over illicit enrichment. Galeano thinks he was always a troublesome judge for the higher powers. The paradox is that his adversaries view him as a judge who bowed to that same power. Another thing left to him from that era is a fatwa: "And let me remind you," Galeano said in trial in 2019, "that the Iranian state not only requested my extradition, but those of us who investigated them were the only recipients of two fatwas, or religious death orders. One was against me, and I can tell you, the other was against Nisman."

The attack has now coloured nearly thirty years of Argentine politics. But in the first thirty days the mystery appeared to be solved. Some of the things discovered in that month (from 18 July to 18 August 1994) remain pillars of the investigation: the existence of a bomb in a Renault Trafic; the Trafic's history, including the chapter with Telleldín as a local connection; even the probable responsibility of Hezbollah and certain officials in the Iranian government. Then everything seemed to flounder, and the legal case sank into a mire from which it still has not managed to escape. I asked Galeano what happened.

"The problem is that when you start looking deeper into matters of private and public corruption, there is an endless chain of factors and proving any one of them is complex," he explains. "I wanted to know the truth about what happened. And we did find out the truth, we did find out the truth ... but it isn't easy to bring international terrorists into a courtroom. And sticking your nose into the Buenos Aires Province police ... those kinds of things always bring problems."

The AMIA's lawyer, Bronfman, wrote in his book that the labour involved in the case was "monumental" and that "not only was a great deal clarified, but nothing was left uninvestigated". Memoria Activa indicated the opposite: "Former judge Galeano is one of the people responsible for the fact that, more than twenty-one years after the attack, the relatives of victims and Argentine society do not know what happened on 18 July 1994."

> "I was thirty-four when the case came to me ... even my staff were all twenty, twenty-two"

Evening is falling. The former judge's face is now half illuminated by the yellow light of a desk lamp. "I was thirty-four years old when the case came to me. With more experience I would have handled it differently, even my staff were all twenty, twenty-two, and we had to take charge in a matter of terrorism in Argentina without police support. Or with the appearance of police support, with the appearance of intelligence support, but each of them had their own agenda. And I thought that when they blow up a building in the middle of the city of Buenos Aires, the capital of Argentina, what would interest all of us most is being on the same side, and looking for a solution to the problem – something that clearly did not happen."

Argentina: in union and liberty. That is my country's motto.

We speak a while longer. But one would need countless hours to get to the bottom of Galeano's words – to explore the elusive complexity of the case, and his role in it. Eventually he accompanies me to the door. It is a heavy, armoured door. When it shuts, I understand that the man has been left alone with his past once more.

17.

Detroit, 18 September 2005. The prosecutor, Nisman, arrives in the city to interrogate two Lebanese men: Hassan and Abbas, from the Berro family. The first is forty-two and has six children. Of the second we know only that he is twenty-seven and a dental technician. Nisman – who is now leading the investigation into the attack – wants to speak with them because, two years earlier, Mossad had sent the SIDE what everyone was hoping to discover: the name of the suicide bomber who drove the van. (Another account indicates that the SIDE obtained the name thanks to a CIA informant, a former member of Hezbollah who was interrogated by Argentine agents in Uruguay.)

The name was Ibrahim Hussein Berro. A young Lebanese man of barely twenty-one, he was a member of Hezbollah who travelled from Lebanon to Paraguay and, along with three other men in the organisation, to Argentina. (In March 2003, Judge Galeano had ordered the arrest of those three and, in a legal filing, introduced the theory about Berro, though he warned that it was also possible the man had died in southern Lebanon. Without hesitation, Mullen told me: "The suicide bomber was Berro.")

The FBI located the Berro brothers – the eldest, Hassan, had moved to the United States in 1985, followed by his brother Abbas in 1996. So Nisman flies to Detroit with his deputy prosecutor as well as a SIDE chief: the director-general of operations for the past twenty-five years, a counterintelligence specialist, the head of Section 85, known by the names Jaime Stiuso, Horacio Stiuso, Antonio Stiuso, Antonio Stiles, Aldo Stiles and Jaime Stiles, but born Antonio Horacio Stiuso – a collector of other people's secrets who is feared by a multitude of politicians and admired by some as well. Among his admirers is the Argentine president at the time, Néstor Kirchner, who introduced him to Nisman as "the man who knows most about the AMIA case in the world".

A special prosecution unit had been created for the AMIA case the previous year, 2004, with thirty staff and seven secretaries. Nisman had been put in charge – a Jewish prosecutor who was gradually refining his appearance, adopting an American style that added another layer of mystique to the case. Stiuso, a spy with an aptitude for investigation and good contacts among his counterparts around the world, would become his indispensable ally.

Many of the leads that had guided the investigation for ten years had been abandoned. Galeano had fallen; the SIDE department that had organised Telleldín's payment – Sala Patria – had fallen; the lead involving the police officers had fallen. But with Nisman and Stiuso, a new era has begun: they need to capture the Iranians once and for all, and this entails trips across the world, judicial lobbying and contact with Interpol. And so Nisman and Stiuso are in Detroit, ready to return to Buenos Aires with a great revelation. The SIDE's information indicated that Berro had arrived in Buenos Aires from the Triple Frontier prior to the attack, accompanied by a resident of Paraguay named Saad, and that he had stayed for a few days in a house belonging to suspected members of Hezbollah. Then Berro had blown himself up. But the suspected suicide bomber's brothers refuse to confirm anything.

One claims to have been with Berro a week or two before his death, which he says occurred on 9 September 1994 (that is, months after the AMIA attack). They believe he was killed during an Israeli attack on the Lebanese town of Talloussa. Berro had left his school and his friends behind in 1989, they said, and had begun disappearing for several days at a time after another of their brothers died in a fire. Suddenly the boy was going to training camps, which he entered with the help of his brother Alí, a medic for Hezbollah. An explosion had left him lame and with damage to his lungs. But when Nisman and Stiuso hear that Berro's body never turned up in Talloussa, they seize on this information, repeating and repeating it until Hassan loses patience: "I can't stand any more of you! I don't know what's going on!"

In the end, one of the brothers agrees to take a DNA test to compare against a small tissue sample held in Argentina, believed to belong to the driver of the van.

The result is negative.

Nisman believes that the brothers are either lying or they have been lied to about Berro's death in Talloussa. And that the test is not conclusive. Two months later, in November, he announces that the suicide driver has been identified. He says it was a member of Hezbollah and exhibits two photographs that resemble the facial composite made by the federal police in 1994 based on the description of a witness who saw the Trafic. This witness – María Nicolasa Romero – now seems to recognise the suicide bomber.

The excitement lasts less than twenty-four hours. Abbas Berro – the younger brother – denies all of it in an interview on an Argentine radio show. He says that investigators had showed him a photo of the suspected suicide bomber but it was not his brother. "We're certain that our brother didn't have anything to do with the attack," he says.

Nisman takes the predictable hit from the failure of his long-awaited announcement. Berro disappears from the case. Today that great revelation is no more than a conjecture, impossible to prove.

18.

Nisman did not appeal the acquittal of Telleldín and the police officers in 2004 – and Nisman was not accused by that tribunal. Though he had not taken part in the initial investigations, he had been working on the case since 1997 and was in the loop about everything, or nearly everything. He could have been accused – as Mullen was – for not disclosing the payment to Telleldín, and for other irregularities. Nisman said that he had not appealed because of his republican ideals, but the rumour is that he negotiated a deal with one of the three judges: Nisman would not question the sentence and they would not denounce him. Regardless, the leadership of the Jewish community and some of the victims' relatives appealed the ruling, and the matter made its way to the Supreme Court. Years later, in 2009, the court threw out the acquittal and ordered that Telleldín be tried once again – and the police officers too, though only in regard to extortion, not the attack.

"I spoke with Nisman several times," Telleldín told me. After the Supreme Court's 2009 ruling, for example, he and his lawyer went to see Nisman to request a document certifying that there had been no new evidence since 2004. At first, Nisman said he would give it to him. Then later he said no: "I can't give it to you because they'll crucify me, the victims' relatives will kill me." That's how many remember him: a frank person with a deadlocked case.

Nisman did not add many new discoveries to the file. "He never worked," Diana Wassner told me. But perhaps he served a different role. What he did, according to the journalist Gerardo Young in his book *Código Stiuso* (*The Stiuso Code*), was to keep the case alive when it seemed to be hopelessly sinking. Between March and August of 2003, Judge Galeano, still in office, called for the international arrest of twelve officials (including former ambassador Hadi Soleimanpour, the cultural attaché Mohsen Rabbani, former intelligence minister Ali Fallahian and chief Hezbollah operative Imad Mughniyeh). The former ambassador Soleimanpour was arrested in the United Kingdom; Argentina demanded his extradition, but London refused due to lack of evidence. Sometime later, Galeano was forced to leave the case. With his removal, Interpol cancelled the international arrest warrants he had filed.

Only in 2007 did Nisman manage to get Interpol to put five Iranians back on its red notice list: Fallahian; Rabbani; the former Revolutionary Guards commander Mohsen Rezaei; the former Al-Quds force commander Ahmad Vahidi; and the former third secretary of the embassy in Buenos Aires, Ahmad Reza Asghari. The general accusation made by Nisman, based on information from dissidents in the regime as well as a heap of crosslinked calls between Buenos Aires, the Triple Frontier and the Middle East, stated that the attack had been decided on 14 August 1993, in Mashhad, Iran. It was planned by the supreme religious leader, Ali Khamenei; the president, Ali Rafsanjani; the minister of foreign affairs, Akbar Velayati; Fallahian; Rabbani; and the third secretary of the embassy, Ahmad Reza Asghari. Not all of Nisman's remaining requests were granted by Interpol. He also called for the arrest of a Lebanese Hezbollah member (Samuel Salman El Reda or Salman Raouf Salman) and of the head of Hezbollah's Foreign Relations Unit (Imad Fayez Mughniyeh).

These accusations earned Nisman a fatwa.

One might suppose that a fatwa is an occupational hazard, and that a prosecutor going after terrorism would barely notice it. But the anonymous threats Nisman habitually received were eroding his mental health. Recently separated from his wife, alone in an apartment in Puerto Madero, armed with an unhackable phone, protected by bodyguards whom one can never trust in the end, a junkie for intelligence reports, the man was living in fear.

That same year, 2007, Néstor Kirchner ended his presidency. His wife, Cristina Fernández, succeeded him. In 2009, she issued a demand at the United Nations for Iran to cooperate and turn over the accused – she was supporting Nisman's investigation. Néstor Kirchner died from a heart attack in 2010. It was sudden and shocking: he was popular. In 2011, Cristina Fernández won reelection. More than ever, she leaned

Nisman was going to war against his old ally the president, against the left, and against Iran

on her regional allies, Brazil's Lula and Venezuela's Hugo Chávez. Chávez was a good friend of Iran. Was Chávez the one who asked Fernández to leave the Iranians alone?

In 2013 she offered a treaty: let's forget Interpol, let's hold a trial together in neutral territory, let's dispense with the manhunt. And, more importantly, let's start trading again. Let's be pragmatic. That was not how it was presented, but you could read between the lines. It was enshrined in a memorandum of understanding, which the Argentine and Iranian diplomats signed in Addis Ababa and which the Argentine congress ratified after a prickly debate. The official rationale was that the case was paralysed after nineteen years of impunity.

Suddenly, the red notices and even the investigation were no use. For Nisman and Stiuso, this was checkmate.

Two decades without justice. Dozens of petitions, drafted by Jewish organisations and opposition parties, were lodged at the federal courts to halt the memorandum. On 14 January 2015, the prosecutor drafted a very serious allegation: he said that the memorandum was a cover-up by the president, and that a form of parallel diplomacy had been established to negotiate with Iran, involving congresspeople, members of the Argentine Islamic community, Iranian officials and radicalised leftist activists with ties to Iran, a country with which they sympathised because they had the United States as a common enemy. Nisman was accusing almost everyone. But the most stunning thing was Cristina Fernández de Kirchner's inclusion.

The prosecutor was due to present his complaint before congress on 19 January. He was going to war against his old ally the president, against the left, and against Iran. He had got himself into a titanic battle.

At that time he was on a trip to Europe with his daughter, who was turning fifteen. "I had to suspend my trip with my daughter and come back early," he wrote in a WhatsApp message to a group of friends.

> You can guess what that means. But sometimes in life you don't choose the moment, simply, things happen and it is for a reason. What I'm going to do now was going to happen anyway. It was already decided. I've been preparing for this for a while, but I didn't imagine it coming so soon. It would take too long to explain now, as you already know, things happen, period. That's life. The rest is allegorical. Some of you will know what I'm

talking about, others can imagine something, and others will have no idea. Until a little while from now. I'm gambling a lot on this. Everything, I'd say. But I've always made decisions and today won't be the exception. And I'm convinced about doing it. I know it isn't going to be easy. Quite the opposite. But sooner rather than later the truth wins out and I am very confident. I'll do everything within my reach, and more, no matter who I'm facing. Thanks to all of you. There will be justice!! Oh. And to be clear I haven't gone crazy or anything like that. In spite of everything, I'm better than ever. Ha ha ha ha ha ha.

The night before his presentation to congress he reviewed the complaint and chatted with an anti-Kirchnerist representative. Then he opened his computer, pulled up his email inbox, read the newspapers *Página/12*, *Clarín*, *La Nación*, *Infobae* and *Perfil* online, and went on Instagram to look at pictures of a woman he had slept with four days before. At some point he stopped on a column on *Infobae* about dying and coming back. It was the story of Mellen-Thomas Benedict, an artist from the United States who claimed to have been dead for an hour and a half in 1982. The artist spoke of a psychedelic journey, leading Nisman to google the word "psychedelia". Maybe he read about alterations to the perception of time and the sense of identity. And then he closed the computer.

We lose him for a few hours. We do not know anything of him now. Where is he? He is not responding to phone calls. This is unusual. His mother worries and decides, very late, to go to his apartment. There she finds him lying unconscious in the bathroom, in a t-shirt and shorts, spattered with blood, a gun next to him and a hole in the side of his head, above his right ear.

It was a single shot, .22 calibre.

His mother called for an ambulance, and with the ambulance came the police, and with the police came the legal authorities, and with the legal authorities came the secretary of security. The scene filled with people. It was complete chaos because everyone knew that Nisman was, on that day, the most important person in Argentina. And the most important person in Argentina was lying there with a bullet in his head.

When the sun rose, the news was filled with nothing else. "It was a tragic day," says Bronfman, the AMIA's lawyer. "I thought the country I had been born in and where I grew up no longer existed."

Theories abounded: Nisman was killed by the SIDE, the CIA, Mossad, a Venezuelan-Iranian commando, some subordinate of the president; Stiuso betrayed him … But the government supported the theory of a suicide: the ministers said the complaint was so shameful that Nisman could not defend it, and he had chosen a bullet instead.

"When Nisman dies, I go on the Gato Silvestre TV show," Telleldín says. "They ask: what do you think? I say: the truth is, if an [intelligence] agent from Argentina had assassinated him, they would have left their [ID] card, because they're useless. Neither the United States nor Israel likes Cristina Kirchner, because it's a leftist government, so if he was assassinated, it was by the CIA or Mossad. His dead body was worth more for damaging her in the 2015 elections; it wasn't worth anything for the AMIA business because nothing had been achieved."

Telleldín remembers one of the mysteries in the case: a woman who turned up dead in front of Nisman's place, having been set on fire, in the early morning, almost a month after his death. The medical examiners could determine only that the woman was between forty and fifty years old and was 1.65 metres tall. The fire had taken her name with it – she was never identified. Today the case is listed as "death due to uncertain criminal causes" and has been shelved. Some conspiratorial minds read this as a key: "Nisman liked girls," Telleldín says. "If they got in, they got in using a girl and then assassinated her. That's how the services operate." But he ultimately believes that the prosecutor took his own life. "They were about to dismiss him because there were leads he didn't investigate so as to cover for the SIDE."

Among the many senseless details in the case is the weapon used: an old Bersa pistol that a trustworthy computer technician, Diego Lagomarsino, had loaned to Nisman. "He asked me for it because he said he was afraid for his life," Lagomarsino explained. No one understands whether he is part of the plot or a victim (he has been investigated as an accomplice to the murder, perhaps unfairly). And while the gun's origins were confusing everyone, the case became unsolvable; it became charged with political significance and divided public opinion. It was debated in offices, in cafés, in taxis and especially on television. During that first week, many people went out into the streets demanding justice – on one rainy day, they booed the government from under their umbrellas.

"There were a thousand reasons for him to commit suicide and a thousand reasons for someone to kill him"

Many people grew concerned after this new turn in the AMIA case. For example, Luis Czyzewski and Ana María Blugerman, the parents of Paola Czyzewski. On 18 July 1994, Paola had accompanied her mother to the AMIA. It was her first time there: she was studying Economic Sciences, and her mother, who was an external auditor for the AMIA, thought it would be a good idea to help her with her work. At 9.53, the fatal hour, Paola was on the ground floor getting coffee and her mother was on another floor. "I live with the guilt of having brought her there and having survived without a scratch," her mother recently said. Paola had turned twenty-one on 14 August 1993, the day that, according to Nisman's investigations, a council of Iranian officials in Mashhad ordered the AMIA attack.

Paola's parents believe Nisman was murdered.

"There were a thousand reasons for him to commit suicide and a thousand reasons for someone to kill him," the former prosecutor Mullen tells me with a certain gloom.

In 2017, a judge concluded that Nisman's death was a crime. According to an expert witness from the National Gendarmerie, the prosecutor had been sedated with ketamine and hit in the nose, the liver and the legs. One of the assassins held him to the floor with a knee and the other shot him. But this testimony has been much disputed. In January 2021, the government of Alberto Fernández – whose vice-president is Cristina Fernández (they are not related) – provided other expert testimony from the ministry of security. The government sought to demonstrate that the case had an anti-Kirchnerist political motivation. The expert report indicated that the Gendarmerie acted improperly at the scene, and that Nisman was alone in the bathroom when the bullet impacted.

In the end, the memorandum of understanding with Iran was never implemented. In November 2022, Paola's father, along with other relatives of victims, demanded in a petition that Cristina Kirchner and the rest of the accused be investigated again, bringing back the original complaint. But Nisman's report fell into oblivion.

19.

The framed portrait shows Nisman in his finest era: when the special prosecution unit was his and the president had not yet let go of his hand. When the Iranians were hiding from him and the intelligence services were bringing him information. The portrait stands on a table in the office that for ten years was his. It is not the first thing I see when I arrive – you could say the portrait is just there, between the flag and the books, one more object.

The office is now occupied by Sebastián Basso. He grew up in Mar de Ajó, a beach town quite far from Buenos Aires, and came to the big city to study philosophy. In the end he dedicated himself to the law but never abandoned philosophy, as he tells me with an amiable smile. He appears serene and enjoys the conversation. "There's a great deal of politics in terrorism," he says at one point during our interview, as though searching for the philosophical roots of the AMIA case, "because, ultimately, terrorism challenges the essence of the state …"

After Nisman's death, the office was managed by a triumvirate of prosecutors, but it became unstable. The twenty-fifth anniversary was approaching. In 2018, the head prosecutor brought in Basso – along with another prosecutor named Gonzalo Miranda – because, from his public prosecutor's office in Morón, he had pursued the case of an Argentine citizen kidnapped by ISIS and had taken part in clandestine negotiations that secured her freedom. "Now you have to go to the prosecution for the AMIA," his boss told him. It was not a reward.

"I'm a lawyer, not a politician, and I don't have ties with anyone. Not with Memoria Activa, not with the AMIA, not with anyone, and therefore I'm not going to take sides," Basso says. In fact, Memoria Activa requested his removal because he is a second cousin of the former judge Riva Aramayo, the woman who negotiated with Telleldín in prison. But Basso uses the word "neutral" to describe himself.

When he arrived, he devoted himself to reviewing the file and discarding what could no longer be of use. "I didn't do it alone," he tells me. "People think that when you arrive, you start from zero. I didn't start from zero, I'm the continuation of an effort that has always been going."

He sees himself as a craftsman. He is intrigued by the details: it is through them that he seeks to arrive at new conclusions. Now the investigation is aimed at unmasking support for the terrorists in the Triple Frontier, in Brazil and in Panama. And at examining the SIDE materials declassified by the government.

"In this case there is a great deal of misinformation, but it's false that nothing is known about what happened," he continues. He reminds me that it was proved there was a car bomb: a Trafic, which had passed through Telleldín's hands and was driven by someone who disintegrated in the explosion. Some 300 kilograms of ammonium nitrate were used, with a detonator – TNT? – and soil to direct the blast wave. The work of Hezbollah.

And no, the Syria lead does not seem to lead anywhere.

Did Telleldín know that the van was going to become a car bomb? "We aren't going to be able to confirm that," he says. The second trial against Telleldín concluded in 2020 and once again he was acquitted. The ruling is being appealed at the very moment I am writing.

It was proved that the explosion originated with the van and did not come from the dumpster or from inside the building. The prosecutor grows irritated when I ask about the dumpster, and how the story could have gone with a different inquest. "The evidence for the Trafic isn't testimonial, it's scientific evidence," he says. "The material remnants were preserved, they're still there today. There is scientific certainty and judicial certainty – what more do they want? Anyone who wants to doubt it is doing so in bad faith or because they literally refuse to believe anything ... It's doubting the most basic thing!"

There are six Interpol red notices in the case: the Iranians Ali Fallahian (then minister of intelligence); Mohsen Rezaei (head of the Islamic Revolutionary Guard Corps); Ahmad Vahidi (head of the elite Al-Quds Force, now the interior minister); Mohsen Rabbani (cultural attaché at the embassy); and Ahmad Reza Asghari (third secretary at the embassy); as well as Samuel Salman El Reda or Salman Raouf Salman (from Hezbollah).

Others among the accused are Alí Akbar Velayati (Iranian minister of foreign affairs); and Hadi Soleimanpour (Iranian ambassador to Argentina).

The investigation must continue: society demands it and the victims deserve it

And two others are already dead: Akbar Hashemi Bahramani Rafsanjani (the former president of Iran, who died aged eighty-two in Tehran in 2017, officially of a heart attack, though his family believes he was murdered); and Imad Fayez Mughniyeh (head of Hezbollah's Foreign Relations Unit, who was killed by a car bomb in Syria in 2008, reportedly by the CIA and Mossad).

Despite the confusion regarding Telleldín and Galeano and the various local connections, and despite the unsettling and not entirely clear account of the dumpster, the masterminds seem to have been identified – some with more certainty than others – even though they have not been brought to justice. And that, after all, is not nothing.

The thirtieth anniversary is not far off. After so much time, the investigation must continue: society demands it and the victims deserve it. "The role of the public prosecutor's office is to go through everything that's left to be done as rapidly as possible," Basso says. "The AMIA case did not reach that point. There are still possibilities to investigate." But it is not possible to convict the accused if they are not present in Argentina.

Linetzky, the president of the AMIA, had mentioned the possibility of a trial in absentia. "There are serious legal systems, like those of Italy and France, in which justice in absentia is legislated," he told me. "The president of the nation [Alberto Fernández], who is a jurist, told us he's in favour of justice in absentia and believes it should be part of Argentina's legislation, but he doesn't think it applies for the AMIA case, since the penal code can't be applied retroactively unless it benefits the defendant, which wouldn't be happening here."

20.

The AMIA case file reached colossal proportions and was digitised: 720 sections; 146,000 sheets or pages; 422 binders; 775 phone lines tapped; 134 people suspected of having some form of involvement in the attack, of whom forty-two remain under investigation. Seventy people had inquiries dismissed by prosecutors and eight were officially acquitted. Probably it is the largest file in Argentina.

I ask the prosecutor if I can see that file. I think about everything it contains and everything it conceals. About its testimonies and its rulings. About the dust, the money and the blood that run through its pages. I want to see that inconceivable, eternal monstrosity – is it possible? It is possible, yes, of course. The file can be found in this public prosecutor's office. Basso invites me to see it and take a tour of the office, two things that are in fact the same because the file occupies the entire space, expanding into every corner and every room. The file is the office, and the office is the file.

We make our way through a few rooms of metal shelves on which rest the archives and objects from the summary proceedings. In one room, on the wall, there is a chart showing Iranian terrorists. In another room, a map of Floresta, the neighbourhood where many of the suspects live, each of their houses marked. In a little room I see a safe. In a narrow office there are folders from the SIDE that are being declassified. One page has been left on the desk: it is written in Farsi or Arabic. I have no way of knowing if it is a diamond or a lump of coal.

> *The file is the office, and the office is the file*

We advance, room by room, and the prosecutor Basso is talking to me now but I am in a daze, trying to see everything together, trying to capture it in my mind, and Telleldín and Galeano appear to me, not as I have known them but rather their skulls, and we walk ahead and see almost no one; Basso smiles and says that the prosecutor's office is under renovation, just as the AMIA was on 18 July 1994, right before the explosion, and everything seems a bit confused, and standing before a long table Basso explains how they hold their team meetings here, and I wonder if this was the very table where Nisman informed his people that he had a fatwa on his head and warned: if they can, they'll kill us all ...

Today there is no team meeting, only blurry figures who pass and keep going. And with two more steps we finish the tour and appear in the doorway of Basso's office, right where we began.

The prosecutor's office made a complete revolution under my feet. Then I realise that the floor is designed in a circle: the office is in fact a snake biting its own tail, a snake made of paper, born to die again and again in mysterious cycles. The misery and justice, the darkness and light of a nation have been held captive here, inside these archives, inside these documents. Perhaps forever. ≡

History

Madrid, 1991: When enemies finally met

Ian Black

Ian Black was a former Middle East correspondent and Middle East editor at *The Guardian* and a former contributing editor at The Jewish Quarterly. He died on 22 January 2023 from a rare neurological disease. This piece was completed shortly before his death. Characteristically, he suggested an early deadline because he was concerned about his failing health. His wife, Helen Harris, writes:

When Ian wrote this piece, his right hand no longer worked and he typed the article mainly with the forefinger of his left hand. At that point he could no longer speak and we communicated with a text-to-speech app that spoke with a BBC newsreader's voice rather than Ian's own. His mobility was failing. But the writing and thinking part of his brain carried on whirring away till the end.

On 30 October 1991, a landmark Middle Eastern event began in Madrid. It was the first ever public meeting between Israel, Jordan and the Palestinians, co-sponsored by the United States and the Soviet Union. But the beautiful location was more impressive than the conference itself, which produced little immediate progress in resolving what was – and remains – one of the most intractable conflicts in the world.

Because of that failure, the conference has been largely forgotten, only vaguely remembered by the diplomats who were there and the journalists who covered it – including myself. Yet historians who have researched it over the past three decades tell a more complex story: its longer-term influence on later Arab–Israeli negotiations is too often ignored.

Geopolitically, these were rapidly changing times: the fact that the conference was arranged by the US and the USSR – former rivals for global power – speaks volumes. In March 1991, President George H.W. Bush told the United States Congress: "The time has come to put an end to the Arab–Israeli conflict." Bush's declaration was followed by eight months of intensive shuttle diplomacy by Secretary of State James Baker.

The co-chairs were Bush and Soviet president Mikhail Gorbachev, who had survived a coup attempt that August and was flattered to be invited. It was attended by Israeli, Egyptian, Syrian and Lebanese delegations, as well as, crucially, a joint Jordanian-Palestinian delegation. For the first time, all parties to the Arab–Israeli conflict had gathered for direct negotiations.

Bush and Gorbachev tried hard to sustain the fiction of equality, but their media appearances underlined the imbalance in their status. Bush represented the world's only superpower, while Gorbachev had the humiliation of being asked – by an *Izvestia* correspondent – to what extent he was still in charge of his country.

The four-day gathering began formally in the magnificent Palacio Real. Preparations went smoothly except for a spat over whether the hosts would remove an enormous oil painting of Charles V slaughtering Moors. The conference was held almost exactly 500 years after the conquest of Spain's last Muslim kingdom. In an interview with *El Mundo*, the leader of the Palestine Liberation Organization (PLO), Yasser Arafat, who was in Tunis, called Spain "the most Arab country in Europe".

Everyone recognised that the stakes were high: on the eve of the conference two Israeli settlers were killed and five injured when their bus was raked with gunfire on a lonely West Bank road. They had been on their way to a rally in Tel Aviv to urge the government to stand firm against demands for the surrender of any "administered" or occupied territory.

Bush's description of the participants as "reluctant and uneasy players" was an understatement. "The real work will not happen here in the plenary session, but in direct bilateral negotiations," he declared. From the first day the conference was largely ceremonial and choreographed – it attracted massive media coverage and provided arresting images. Over 5000 journalists covered it. Excitement was most palpable among the droves of Israeli correspondents trying – without great success – to interview their Arab colleagues. Some optimists tried to gain access to the actual delegations. One British journalist faxed an Israeli official describing himself as "the sole legitimate representative" of his magazine, but the jokey reference to the PLO was not appreciated.

In reality, the ban on PLO officials participating was a charade

The immediate regional context mattered a great deal: Saddam Hussein's invasion of Kuwait in August 1990 had boosted Washington's confidence in its ability to influence the Middle East. Syria's president, Hafez al-Assad, had worked with the United States to fight Iraq. Israel had shown restraint in the face of Scud missile fire from Iraq. The support for Saddam from King Hussein of Jordan and Arafat was another factor.

"Baker believed that the US success in assembling an Arab coalition in the Gulf War had bolstered the Arab world's confidence in it," Zalman Shoval, then Israel's ambassador to Washington, wrote later, "at the same time reducing Israel's bargaining power ... and that a suitable background for an initiative on the Israeli–Arab question had been created as a result."

A few weeks after the war ended, Baker visited Cairo, Damascus, Riyadh, Amman and Jerusalem to test the waters with regard to the proposed event. And there were ten additional shuttles.

"The conference," said the carefully worded US–Soviet invitation, "will have no power to impose solutions on the parties or veto agreements made by them. It will have no authority to make decisions for the parties and no ability to vote on issues or results. The conference can only convene with the consent of all the parties."

Direct bilateral negotiations were to begin three days after the opening ceremony. Those parties wishing to attend multilateral negotiations were to convene two weeks afterwards to discuss arms control and regional security, water, environment and economic development. Two tracks were designed for negotiations: one between Israel and Arab states; and one between Israel and the Palestinians, but only as part of a delegation with Jordan. These were based on United Nations Security Council resolutions 242 and 338, which called for an exchange of territory for peace through direct negotiations.

The United States then possessed a rare means of pressure on Jerusalem: Bush resisted an Israeli request for $10 billion in loan guarantees to finance housing for the surge in Russian immigrants. Concerned that the money would finance illegal settlement growth, Washington postponed a decision until February 1992.

From the start, there was not much optimism: a week before the event, Yitzhak Shamir, Israel's Likud prime minister and former Stern Gang leader, announced that he would be leading the delegation rather than his foreign minister, David Levy, ignoring the requirement that all participants be represented by their foreign ministers. The opposition Labour Party accused Shamir of torpedoing peace efforts. The move also pointed to a tough stance being adopted by Israel in response to the increasingly overt role of the PLO, which had been formally excluded from the talks because of American and Israeli opposition. That toxic element provided a lot of tension: Saeb Erekat, a member of the Palestinian delegation, attracted attention by draping a keffiyeh over his suit. Syrian foreign minister Farouk al-Sharaa set the tone by displaying a British Mandate–era "Wanted" photograph of Shamir and calling him a terrorist. Both aroused Baker's visible ire.

In reality, the ban on PLO officials participating was a charade: Israeli representatives knew full well that the organisation's leaders would hold frantic phone conversations from their headquarters in Tunis with Palestinians attending the sessions. Nabil Shaath, a close adviser to Arafat, was in Madrid and repeatedly briefed journalists. Hanan Ashrawi, the official spokesperson, always took care to stress the connection with the PLO. Her colleague Faisal Husseini, from East Jerusalem, quipped that "the suit that the American peace team tailored for the negotiations does not fit my body".

The very fact that there were Palestinian representatives was perceived as a sign of the success of the intifada, which had erupted nearly four years earlier. "For the first time, we shall sit across the table from our enemies," wrote the Palestinian-American academic Edward Said, "in a negotiation that is neither secret nor local, but international, relatively open, and held under the auspices of the major powers."

No real negotiations were carried out at the conference itself; each delegation head instead used the podium to make political points to audiences at home. One memorable moment came when the chairman of the Palestinian Red Crescent Society, Dr Haidar Abdel-Shafi, made a touching, quietly spoken speech. A veteran supporter of the PLO, he had spent three years in an Israeli prison. "We seek neither an admission of guilt after the fact, nor vengeance for past iniquities," he said, "but rather an act of will that would make a just peace a reality."

Shamir spoke of the need to "build confidence" and "remove the danger of confrontation". At the same time, he appeared to rule out exchanging land for peace. "The issue is not territory but our existence," he said. No one applauded, but no one walked out either. Abdel-Shafi, by contrast, spoke practically, saying Palestinians would accept a "transitional stage provided that interim arrangements are not transformed into permanent status" – offering at least a start for the bilateral process. Shamir, who was not observant, flew home in time for Shabbat on Friday, 1 November, underlining his overall negative approach.

Abdel-Shafi played well on deep divisions in the Jewish state. "We have seen you anguish over the transformation of your sons and daughters into instruments of a blind and violent occupation," he told Israelis, "and we are sure that at no time did you envisage such a role for the children you thought would forge your future." Israel's deputy foreign minister, Binyamin Netanyahu, excelled at his own art of advocacy by scoffing at Abdel-Shafi's "flowery language". Netanyahu – dubbed the "Abba Eban of the CNN era" – turned the conference into a fount of Israeli *hasbara*.

On 3 November, Israeli–Palestinian negotiations began, away from the stilted posturing of the Palacio Real. The location was the more modest Palacio de Parcent, a justice ministry building in central Madrid. A five-strong Israeli delegation, headed by cabinet secretary Elyakim Rubinstein; six Jordanians, led by King Hussein's adviser, Abdel Salam al-Majali; and five Palestinians, led by Abdel-Shafi. "Businesslike" was the adjective most used about their meeting.

But endless wrangling delayed Israel's bilateral encounters with the Syrians and Lebanese. After the Lebanese ended their first round, the Syrians finally sat down with the Israelis more than twelve hours later than scheduled.

Netanyahu expressed "astonishment" at the Syrians' failure to turn up at the time and venue agreed with the United States. "These are games," he added. "If you're serious about peace, be there at the designated time, at the designated place."

Following Madrid, Israeli, Syrian, Jordanian and Palestinian representatives continued to meet for bilateral talks in Washington, DC, and multilateral talks commenced in Moscow in 1992. Yet by 1993, the Washington talks had become deadlocked and were overtaken by secret Israeli–Palestinian and Israeli–Jordanian negotiations, which produced the Israeli–Palestinian Declaration of Principles (the Oslo Accord) of September 1993 and the Israeli–Jordanian peace treaty of October 1994. Much of the latter treaty was agreed during Shamir's term as prime minister, though it was signed by his successor, Labour's Yitzhak Rabin.

"The Madrid Conference has not been granted its proper place in history"

Madrid was clearly less significant than the Egyptian–Israeli peace treaty of 1979 and Oslo. But thirty years later, perceptions about its importance have begun to change. "The Madrid Conference has not been granted its proper place in history," Rubinstein told *Haaretz* in October 2021.

It was the first table around which Israel, Jordan and the Palestinians sat openly. There were a lot of meetings before that … but this time – symbolized by the photograph of me shaking hands with my Jordanian and Palestinian counterparts – a new era began, diplomatically open, in frameworks of negotiations that never existed before.

Ashrawi has also characterised Madrid as a "game-changer", and Yossi Beilin, back then a Meretz leader, told a thirtieth-anniversary webinar that characterising Madrid as a failure is "unfair". "I think it helped a lot to actually enable us to create a better atmosphere in the Middle East," said Beilin. "The Oslo agreement would not have happened without Madrid, and peace between Israel and Jordan would not have happened without Oslo. We didn't achieve all that we really wanted to, but the modest achievements were very, very important, and changed the face of the Middle East."

Community

Remembering Salonica, capital of the Diaspora

Rena Molho

Salonica is the central metropolis of the Balkan Peninsula. Due to its strategic position on the ancient Roman road Via Egnatia, the city joins the West (Rome) with the East (Constantinople/Istanbul). Its port in the Thermaic Gulf is the main outlet of the Macedonian hinterland to the Aegean Sea and the Mediterranean. For centuries it harboured the largest Jewish community in the world and served as a beacon for the Jewish Diaspora. This is why the city was known as the "Jerusalem of the Balkans".

Founded in 315 BCE, Salonica (then called Thessaloniki) has been governed by many peoples in its rich 2300-year history, yet has always been home to a Jewish community. During the Ottoman rule from 1492 to 1912, the city's Jewish community expanded and flourished. Its port was closed on Sabbath and on Jewish holidays, and both Jews and non-Jews spoke Judeo-Spanish (Ladino). At the end of the nineteenth century, Greek journalist Christos Christovassilis described Salonica as an "ocean of Jews" (εβραιο-ωκεανόν). He had difficulty finding a Greek shop as he couldn't understand a word of the language spoken.

The first Jews who settled in Thessaloniki in 315 BCE had been given their freedom by Alexander the Great. Favourable conditions, which allowed them to practise their religion and maintain their culture, led to a significant migration of Jews to Macedonia, particularly during the Roman subjugation of Palestine.

The Ottoman conquest of Macedonia in 1430 was followed by an influx of European Jews, most of whom had been expelled from Spain. Salonica was left with just 2000 inhabitants, but the 20,000 Spanish Jews who settled in the city in 1492 played a crucial role in its revival. They were active in international trade, finance, medicine and pharmacy, and their knowledge of foreign languages and Judeo-Spanish helped them to conduct commerce in other cities where Spanish Jews lived. Among them were craftsmen who introduced new skills to the city, such as the manufacturing of arms, gunpowder and textiles.

By the turn of the sixteenth century, Salonica had 29,000 citizens, 50 per cent of them Sephardi Jews. The new settlers gave Salonica an international character and made it the second-most important port in the Ottoman Empire, after Istanbul. Salonica had become an unusual phenomenon in modern Jewish history – a city whose life was defined by its Jews.

In the sixteenth century, considered the golden age of Salonica, the Sephardim established libraries, an important Talmudic Academy, a printing press (1527) and a conservatory for Jewish religious singing (*beit sefer le piyyutim*). They also established thirty-one synagogues or congregations, each named after the geographical origin of its flock, such as Provincia, Mayorca, Castilia, Catalan, Aragon, Italia and Sicilia.

The Spanish Jews were more numerous and better educated than the local Romaniote (Greek-speaking) and Ashkenazi (Yiddish-speaking) Jews who had arrived after 1376, and soon these older communities were assimilated by the Spanish Jews. From the late 1400s until the middle of the twentieth century, Judeo-Spanish was the community's primary language. Manolis Andronikos, the famous Greek archaeologist who discovered Vergina, the site of the ancient capital of Macedonia, and Michalis Tsitsiklis, a well-known criminal lawyer, both spoke Judeo-Spanish with my father-in-law, the bookseller Solomon Molho. All of my father Isaac Bensussan's colleagues in the Ladadika market spoke the language too.

Early in the nineteenth century, the economic and cultural life of the Jewish community began to flourish, following the establishment of popular and vocational schools by the *Alliance Israélite Universelle*. This organisation was created in Paris in 1860 with the goal of emancipating Ottoman Jews through secular education, and was active in most Ottoman urban centres. Salonica then acquired a class of skilled artisans and specialised workers. Between 1878 and 1914, the Allatini family created the biggest flour mill in the Balkans and an important brick factory. Other Salonica Jews created breweries, soapworks and silk-worm nurseries, carpet- and shoe-making factories and several large tobacco workshops.

For the Zionists, Salonica was a model of the kind of Jewish society they wished to build

Nevertheless, the vast majority of the Jews in Salonica were poor. By the turn of the twentieth century the community administration was supporting 6000 of the city's 13,000 Jewish families, who were either unemployed or working as artisans, peddlers and menial workers, mostly in the seafaring trades as porters, boatmen and fishermen. No other Jews in the Diaspora were exercising this trade: in fact, in 1910, David Ben-Gurion and Yitzhak Ben-Zvi – the future prime minister and president of Israel – who had visited the community, brought fifteen of Salonica's Jewish boatmen and fishermen to Palestine to break the Arab monopoly of these trades in Yafo and Akko. Some of them returned to Salonica, but those who stayed were joined in 1932 by 10,000 Salonica Jewish refugees, who came to Palestine to man the new port of Haifa. According to Ze'ev Jabotinsky, Salonica was a model of the kind of Jewish society the Zionists wished to build.

In 1910 Salonica's port was renovated and the city entered modernity. The creation of banks – mainly by the Muslims and Jews, but also by the Greeks – contributed to the city's economic growth. The liberal spirit that culminated in the Young Turk movement (1908) enabled the ethnic minorities to create their first cultural and political associations. The most impressive organisation in Salonica, created in 1909 by a group of local Jews, was the Socialist Workers' Federation, which became the most important workers' union in the Ottoman Empire. In 1918 its Jewish general secretary, Avraam Benaroya, helped to found the Socialist Labour Party of Greece (SEKE) in Athens.

Between 1865 and 1940, more than fifty Jewish newspapers were published in the city, mostly in Judeo-Spanish but also in Turkish, French and Greek, representing all political stripes.

In 1913, following the Balkan Wars, Greece annexed Salonica, cutting it off from its Macedonian hinterland. The city lost its commercial importance and became a border town in the Greek state. The World Zionist Organization, however, urged the Jewish community to give its allegiance to the Greek government since it had kept its promise of fair treatment of the Jewish population.

In 1923, the Asia Minor catastrophe – the Greco-Turkish War that ended Greece's presence in Asia Minor – resulted in the arrival of 120,000 Greek refugees and reduced the importance of the Jewish community. During the interwar period, the Jewish community represented only 20 per cent of the city's population – vastly less than at its peak.

But it was the invasion of the Nazis in 1941 that decimated Europe's most ancient Jewish community. The Nazis murdered 96 per cent of the community's 50,000 members and destroyed its cultural wealth and monuments. Today, the Salonica Jewish community has fewer than 1000 members, not many of whom speak Judeo-Spanish or Ladino. Greek is the first language of the community. Nevertheless, those who remain are active in preserving the memory of their culture through exhibitions, concerts, conferences and guided tours to the remaining Jewish sites. The community has three Orthodox synagogues, one elementary school, an old people's home, a Jewish club and a small Jewish museum (founded in 2000), soon to be replaced by a Holocaust Museum commemorating Salonica's Jewish presence.

Jewish Salonica, light unto the Diaspora, has a glorious past – but its future is precarious. ≡

Reviews

Justice and the Holocaust
James McAuley

Come to This Court and Cry: How the Holocaust Ends
Linda Kinstler
Bloomsbury (UK)/PublicAffairs (US)

In 1982, the acclaimed historian Yosef Hayim Yerushalmi published *Zakhor: Jewish History and Jewish Memory*, a slim volume of four lectures he had given some years before at the University of Washington in Seattle.

The book, a scant 144 pages from start to finish, was almost instantly recognised as one of the most important meditations on Jewish history written after the war. Indeed, *Zakhor* is now a canonical text in the field, a fixture on graduate syllabi and an essential reference point for scholars of memory. But Yerushalmi's masterpiece appeared at a time when defining and shaping the memory of the Holocaust was an urgent mission of Jewish academia and public institutions – President Ronald Reagan's visit to the Bitburg cemetery followed *Zakhor*'s publication by three years; Germany's bitter *Historikerstreit* debates followed it by four. Against that backdrop, here was a succinct look at the crucial place of memory in Jewish tradition, religious and intellectual alike. "What were the Jews to remember, and by what means?" This became a foundational inquiry for Yerushalmi, who notes that *zakhor*, the Hebrew verb meaning "to remember", appears in the Hebrew Bible no fewer than 169 times. In Jewish history and thought, the memory question is not merely an essential question but the source of all questions – in other words, the only question.

One of Yerushalmi's most memorable lines – "Is it possible that the antonym of 'forgetting' is not 'remembering', but justice?" – both begins and ends journalist and historian Linda Kinstler's extraordinary new book, *Come to This Court and Cry: How the Holocaust Ends*, a profoundly beautiful contemplation of family and country, law and literature, fact and truth. On one level, Kinstler is examining the case of Herberts Cukurs, the so-called "Latvian Lindbergh": a beloved national hero before World War II who, during the German occupation, served in the infamous Arajs Kommando, among the most brutal of all the Nazi killing squads. On the heels of the global inflection point in the transmission of Holocaust memory that was the kidnapping, trial and execution of Adolf Eichmann in Jerusalem in 1960–1961, Cukurs, then living in Brazil, was assassinated by Mossad agents in Montevideo, Paraguay, in 1965, accused of involvement in the murders of some 30,000 Jews. But after his death, Cukurs became a case study in post-war narrative fabrication, rehabilitated by local revisionists to the extent that the Latvian government conducted a posthumous investigation into his culpability. He was officially pardoned a few short years ago in a case that Latvian Jewish leaders later appealed.

Kinstler's book is far more personal than her project initially seems. Her parents immigrated to the United States from Soviet Latvia in the late 1980s. Her mother is Jewish, but as a young woman she discovered that her father's father was Boris Karlovics, or Kinstler, who had served in the Arajs Kommando alongside Cukurs. Kinstler describes the surreal experience of wandering into a Riga bookshop in 2016 and discovering her grandfather appearing as a character in a popular spy novel that sought to rehabilitate the reputation of the "Latvian Lindbergh". Before then, she knew only that her grandfather had disappeared after the war; she did not know that he had become a KGB agent, or that he had been a member of the same killing unit responsible for the horrific scenes in which many thousands of Latvian Jews were shot in predominately public places.

"To probe the past is to submit the memory of one's own ancestors to a certain kind of trial. In this case, the trial came to me, or at least the spectre of me," Kinstler writes. The French historian Marie-Claire Lavabre writes that memory is a "*lieu de rencontre*", or meeting place, of stories, testimonies and interpretations. Kinstler learns, poignantly, that her family story is precisely such an intersection.

> These stories – these inheritances, really – come with demands. To receive them is also to inherit a set of obligations and dilemmas: how much to preserve? How much to expose? How much to omit, hide away? How much to reclaim? I started out by studying all of these questions, only to find out that I was already living in them.

There is a chilling scene toward the end of the book when her father sends her, via WhatsApp, a photograph of her grandfather she has never seen before. He is in full German uniform, hair slicked back, *Lettonia* crest patched onto his sleeve. "Maybe I am only now learning which questions to ask, and to discern all that their answers demand."

*

Interrogating such questions – and, more precisely, how certain stories are constructed over others – is the true project of *Come to This Court and Cry*. The bizarre and fantastical tale of Cukurs' abduction and assassination by some of the same Mossad agents who had captured Eichmann has been told before. Most importantly, in 2018, the Israeli journalist Ronen Bergman included the case in *Rise and Kill First: The Secret History of Israel's Targeted Assassinations*, and in 2020 the Irish journalist Stephan Talty published an entire volume about the Cukurs controversy, *The Good Assassin*. Kinstler does not add any new details to our understanding of the Cukurs saga, although her account of what actually happened in Montevideo on 23 February 1965 at about 12.30 p.m. reads like a novel. Her major accomplishment is her unweaving of the various stories that were actively built about the assassination – first by the principal Mossad agent who did the deed, and then, years later, by those who have sought to rehabilitate Cukurs' reputation, and even posthumously to pardon him. This is what makes *Come to This Court and Cry* such a success: it takes nothing for granted, focusing instead on the malleability and the construction of memory, how certain stories are actively chosen, and even fabricated, at the expense of others.

In 1997, the Mossad agent who had killed Cukurs, Yaakov Meidad, published a memoir, defying decades of official Israeli silence about the case, under the pseudonym he had used in the actual operation, Anton Kuenzle (he co-wrote with another agent who used his real name). The book appeared in German in 1998 and in English in 2004, with the title *The Execution of the Hangman of Riga: The Only Execution of a Nazi War Criminal by the Mossad*. Meidad, who died in 2012, was a fascinating character: a German Jew whose parents were both murdered in the Holocaust, he had come to Palestine alone as early as 1934, joined the Israel Defense Forces in 1948 during the War of Independence and then, later, the early iteration of the Israeli intelligence apparatus. He claimed in his memoir that Mossad had no choice but to assassinate Cukurs without a trial, because the West German government's statute of limitations on Nazi war crimes was about to run out in 1965, and also because "none of us had any doubt that this was the just punishment for the sadistic criminal, Herberts Cukurs". Under fierce international pressure, the West German parliament ultimately extended the statute of limitations on prosecuting Nazi crimes; in 1979, it voted 255 to 222 to abolish the statute of limitations altogether.

Nonetheless, as Kinstler makes plain, Meidad's account is "rife with elision, a thicket of contradictions". Among them is his insistence that Cukurs' crimes were on a par with those of Eichmann as a justification for why he wasn't tried, which denied survivors the chance to face the perpetrator in court. "While its basic premise is grounded in fact," Kinstler writes of Meidad's memoir,

> it is hard to understand how one could claim that no historical value, much less testimonial evidence, could be derived from Cukurs's trial, or to argue that none of his surviving victims would have welcomed the opportunity to confront him in court. Cukurs was undoubtedly someone who participated directly in the mass murder of Latvian Jews, but to compare him directly to Eichmann, directly responsible for the death of millions?

Kinstler is pitch perfect when she wonders what this kind of "grotesque comparison" actually implies: it is ultimately "to weigh the deaths of thousands against that of millions, to ask which kind of killing weighs more heavily upon the scale of human sin". She continues:

"Did Eichmann not deserve a violent punishment? Is that not precisely what he received, what his hangman sacrificed his sanity to deliver? Is there not some sense in which sparing Cukurs the embarrassment of a trial and awarding him a quick and spectacular death might also be a form of clemency, a gruesome kind of gift?"

Kinstler is equally critical, and equally incisive, when she unspools other accounts that have sought to salvage Cukurs' reputation. Consider, for instance, her treatment of *You Will Never Kill Him*, the spy novel she spotted in the Riga bookshop that includes a character based on her own grandfather, who serves as a kind of narrative foil to Cukurs. She notes that the genre of the spy novel is a telling choice on the part of the author: spy novels "speak to a base desire for clarity and conservation, an assurance that a small army of agents is somewhere out there, that they not only possess the truth but also nobly shield the rest of us from it." The author, Armands Puče, is a prominent Latvian sports journalist who regularly weighs in on television on all manner of subjects. "It is a vengeful, vicious novel, a ballad of a revanchist nation, an exercise in denial," Kinstler notes, pointing out Puče's reliance on crude antisemitic caricatures like "Jewish gold" and alleged Jewish control over the Latvian economy. "I know who you are," is Puče's sinister greeting to Kinstler when they meet in a Riga coffee shop. Of his novel, he says the following: "It's like fiction, it's like literature, but it's ninety percent based on facts ... You will never kill him – I don't mean Cukurs, I mean this country. You're never going to kill us." Of Cukurs, he has this to say: "In ten or twenty years more, people will accept him ... My generation is starting to ask questions. Why are we just sitting in a corner? Who is responsible for these accusations, especially if there is no evidence of witnesses?"

Nearly every time I have interviewed an antisemite like Puče, and there have been many occasions, I've felt that I have failed both myself and the task at hand. Like Kinstler, I am Jewish and a journalist, but my surname doesn't signal my Jewishness to an interview subject who has a clearly defined conception of "us" and "them". I can never quite find the words, which I tell myself is the journalistic ideal of "objectivity", but is really a blend of embarrassment and conflict aversion. I always end up saying nothing and feeling ashamed. In this instance Kinstler gets her rejoinder, at least on the page. "The thing is," she writes in response to Puče, "it is easy not to find any evidence or witnesses when you yourself have undermined them, omitted them, hidden them away."

Come to This Court and Cry is deftly aware of the ways in which legal and historical judgements depend on narrative for their power. But narratives have to be actively constructed. As Kinstler asks the reader towards the end of her book: "Is it the plot that makes the proof, or the proof that makes the plot?" The answer, of course, is neither: the entire notion of "making a case" begins with a particular objective in mind that is hostile to nuance, contradiction, and facts that do not fit the original objective, while chasing "proof" – definitive proof – is often a fool's errand for both lawyer and historian. This is what makes the Cukurs case so endlessly frustrating, especially the Latvian government's decision in January 2019 to pardon him of any wrongdoing. "There is no evidence that Mr. Cukurs wanted to or did carry out acts that qualify as genocide – that he had taken any action to destroy, in whole or in part, Jewish civilians," the prosecutor's decision read. Throughout the appeal, survivor testimonies were discredited and contextualised, while Cukurs' statements were accepted to the letter. As one of the Jewish plaintiffs seeking to appeal the verdict tells Kinstler, "The logic of the prosecution office seems to be: if the witness did not see someone pulling the trigger, then the person cannot be considered complicit in the genocide."

From the historian's perspective, one of the book's particularly painful passages is when Kinstler's discusses the *corpus delicti* rule in Holocaust cases. The Latvian prosecutor's 2019 decision on Cukurs rested not only, she notes, on the premise that Cukurs' involvement could not be proven beyond any reasonable doubt, but also on the notion that there was not one single body "found dead" that could be verified as having died by Cukurs' hand. But as Kinstler writes so movingly,

> The *body of the crime* was not just one body but millions of bodies. Jews, communists, partisans, Roma – they were neatly ushered to their deaths and either shot, gassed, or buried alive, their remains burned and their graves chemically destroyed. Millions were killed without a trace – their bodies would never be *found dead*.

I thought often of Yerushalmi as I read *Come to This Court and Cry*. There is another line in *Zakhor* that Kinstler doesn't quote but that has always spoken to me. "Let the accumulated facts about the past continue to multiply," Yerushalmi writes. "So that those who need can find that this person did live, those events really took place, this interpretation is not the only one." If narrative is power, its force – and its danger – is permutation.

Come to This Court and Cry is a brilliantly wrought book about family; about how narratives, great and small, are made; about what it means to remember. With another nod to Yerushalmi, Kinstler leaves her readers with a haunting thought. In Hebrew, *zakhor* has the same root as the word *zecher*, which, as Kinstler points out, has a very particular connotation. "To pierce, to puncture," she writes. "To kill." ≡

The books of Ruth

Samantha Ellis

Ruth: A Migrant's Tale
Ilana Pardes
Yale Jewish Lives

It is a paradox, Ilana Pardes writes at the beginning of *Ruth: A Migrant's Tale*, that while the Book of Ruth tells "the most elaborate tale of a woman to be found in the Bible", it is also "astonishingly spare", even "cryptic". To write Ruth's biography, Pardes has had to glean not in the fields like Ruth, trying to support herself and her mother-in-law Naomi, but in the "sparse scenes replete with lacunae" to build up a picture of the migrant woman. Ruth's story is "incredibly rich turf for the exploration of migratory experiences that remain only too relevant today: the acute sense of uprootedness, the struggle to find sustenance in a foreign land, the resilience and audacity that are required in order to survive, the yearnings for home, and the quest for a new beginning".

This is not really biography. Instead, Pardes, a professor of comparative literature at Jerusalem's Hebrew University, analyses Ruth's afterlives in the midrash, in art, novels, films and rituals, looking at how Ruth has been celebrated, maligned, rewritten, reinvented, refracted and appropriated. At its best, this book shows how the maddening gaps in Ruth's story have always offered tantalising invitations to invent.

Pardes is most compelled by the dramatic moment on the road when Naomi, depressed, "empty" and grieving the loss of her husband and sons, tells her two daughters-in-law to go home to their families. Orpah agrees (and has been painted as a villainess for doing so), but Ruth refuses, instead declaring loyalty to Naomi in one of the Bible's best speeches – perhaps its best speech by a woman. Potential immigrants are always tested before being allowed to stay, and Ruth's incandescent words reveal that she knows her loyalty is not enough; she also must commit to Naomi's God and her people, for "foreign wives are accepted as long as they do not violate the monotheistic underpinnings of life and are willing to efface their cultural past". This is a little chilling. I had never noticed that, as Pardes points out, Naomi does not thank Ruth. She does not embrace her. She does not even accept her love; she says nothing. When they get to Bethlehem, she leaves the gleaning to Ruth. Pardes speculates that this may be because Naomi is too old for backbreaking labour, or is lost in grief – but Ruth has lost her husband too. And the reason they scheme to seduce Boaz on the threshing room floor is that the harvest season is over and they need a new plan.

Pardes describes the seduction scene as if it were *A Midsummer Night's Dream*: "The dreamy quality of the encounter makes it all the more nebulous. It is a night of blurred identities, both enchanting and unsettling." The rabbis wrestled with the story. For them, writes Pardes, "every lacuna need[ed] to be probed". The rabbis imagined Boaz asking aloud if Ruth is real or a spirit; they picture her clinging to him "like ivy" and him touching her hair and realising she must be a woman because "spirits have no hair". I have always been captivated by this midrash, and its evidence of the rabbis getting carried away with their exegesis and becoming (rather fabulous) storytellers. I borrowed from it for the title of and big romantic speech in my 2010 play *Cling to Me Like Ivy*, yet another of Ruth's afterlives. Pardes wonders if the rabbis devoted so much energy to this scene because they were struggling with the fact that the mother of King David was a Moabite, and Moabites were always cast as lewd, lascivious, immoral. But I wonder if their focus on Ruth's desires was less about her being foreign than the fact she was a woman.

When the kabbalists read Ruth, they transformed the scene into a moment of mystical union between the Holy One (represented by Boaz) and the *shekhinah*, the feminine aspect of the divine (represented by Ruth). Crucially, however, they saw her as a *shekhinah* in exile. As Pardes movingly notes, they probably found her story of being a stranger in a strange land particularly resonant in light of their experiences in medieval Spain.

But by the seventeenth century, when Ruth started popping up in pastoral paintings, her strangeness began to be erased. She was not depicted as a convert and a foreigner, but as a local, dressed like the other women, often looking beatific, with sunlight gleaming on her hair and the golden sheaves in her arms. Pardes illuminates the way these seemingly inoffensive paintings excited controversy. Gleaning was a hot political topic in both pre-revolutionary and post-revolutionary France, with farmers arguing that the state was trying to get out of giving the poor welfare by insisting that instead they could help themselves to their crops. When Jean-François Millet unveiled *The Gleaners* in 1857, it was criticised for inciting revolution.

Intriguingly, nineteenth-century Orientalist artists also ignored Ruth's status as a migrant. In their paintings, she is dark and alluring – but so are all the other gleaners. Ruth is not depicted as foreign – or, to put it another way, in these paintings everyone is foreign. Pardes astutely traces a line from the Orientalist portraits to later paintings by Zionist artists, for whom Ruth was a migrant, yes, but one who made a happy return to the pastoral landscapes of Israel – not so much gleaning the meagre corners as harvesting the entire field. S.Y. Agnon's novella *In the Prime of Her Life* is an ironic response to those who sought to make Ruth a symbol of homecoming, for Ruth is not coming home; she is going to a place where she is strange, and will continue to be strange even after she has married Boaz and given him a son who will become a king. Pardes quotes the midrash in which David asks God, "How long will they rage against me and say, 'Is he not of a blemished descent? Is he not a descendant of Ruth the Moabitess?'"

Like Pardes, I am thrilled by Julia Kristeva's response to Ruth, namely her idea that "Ruth as foreigner" is there as a reminder "that the divine revelation often requires a lapse, the acceptance of radical otherness". I would love to have learned more about this, and was perplexed that Pardes barely mentions the wonderful 1994 book *Reading Ruth: Contemporary Women Reclaim a Sacred Story*, edited by Judith A. Kates and Gail Twersky Reimer, noting only: "Some of the essays in this volume endorse a feminist-queer outlook on the book of Ruth and see in the relationship of Ruth and Naomi a homo-erotic bond." Perhaps Pardes did not want to repeat her readings of Ruth from her own 1992 volume *Countertraditions in the Bible: A Feminist Approach*, but it seems a shame to devote so little space to some of the fertile, exhilarating, feminist and queer interpretations of Ruth. The Book of Ruth is probably the only book in the Bible that would pass the Bechdel Test, the famous gauge of female representation; films (or other works of art) only pass if they have at least two female characters who have at least one conversation that is not about a man. I would have been interested, too, to read Pardes on Jeanette Winterson's devastating retelling of Ruth in *Oranges Are Not the Only Fruit*, in which her heroine chooses a different path, rejecting her dogmatic mother and her evangelical faith for the young woman she loves.

Going back to the essays in *Reading Ruth*, I remember how startled I was when I first read Vanessa L. Ochs's engagement with the "glitches" in Ruth – for example, when she asks, "What young widow would leave her country and her people and follow her mother-in-law to a place where she will find personal and national salvation through a night spent with an elderly uncle-in-law on a threshing room floor?" Or Avivah Zornberg's *shiur* on how Naomi's expression of bitterness and emptiness is "exactly Kafka's world of existential guilt and despair", which Ruth does her best to counter with *chesed*, kindness. Or Cynthia Ozick on what her religious grandfather owed Ruth:

> Everything, everything. If that woman had not been in the field, my grandfather, three thousand years afterward, would not have been in the study house. She, the Moabite, is why he, when hope is embittered, murmurs the Psalms of David. The track her naked toes make through spice and sweetness, through dodder, vetch, rape, and scabious, is the very track his forefinger follows across the letter-speckled sacred page.

Beside Ozick's lyricism, anyone's writing would seem dry. But Pardes is very strong on her analysis of Michal Ben-Naftali's novel *Chronicle of Separation: On Deconstruction's Disillusioned Love*, written in the voice of a Ruth determined to rewrite her story. In Ben-Naftali's novel, Ruth declares love for Naomi on the road, but is disillusioned, manipulated into seducing Boaz, then forced to hand over her child to Naomi and go. This Ruth wishes she and Naomi had been able to write their story together, but realises this could never be because she is perpetually a stranger, forever other. "Our language, however, was never the same language. I spoke Moabite. You spoke Hebrew. And when I started to speak Hebrew, I stopped speaking the language of my mother and my people." Pardes observes that Ruth's story has shifted meaning in Israel as Israelis have had to confront diversity and otherness. But again, I missed mention of more provocative (and even problematic) readings like the essay by Malawian theologian Fulata Lusungu Moyo, which casts Ruth as a woman who has to sell her body to an older man so that Naomi can regain her dignity through restored property.

In her final chapter, Pardes analyses three American afterlives of Ruth, beginning with Allen Ginsberg's poem *Kaddish*, in which he mourns his mother, whose name was Naomi, as a "Ruth who wept in America", a woman turned mad by migration. After fleeing pogroms in Russia, she had a breakdown and was given shock therapy and a lobotomy. Pardes teases out the way Toni Morrison rewrites, interrogates and riffs on the Book of Ruth in her novel *Song of Solomon* (I particularly enjoyed the observation that the female outcasts in Morrison's novel survive not by gleaning but by running a wine house during Prohibition). Guillermo del Toro, who has described his Catholic upbringing as "morbid", opens his film *The Shape of Water* with scenes from one of Hollywood's old biblical films, Henry Koster's 1960 *The Story of Ruth*. As Pardes writes, all these twenty-first-century Ruths are quintessential outcasts. But I am not sure I agree that each is "a beacon of hope for a culturally diverse United States"; it's certainly hard to find any optimism in the story of Ginsberg's mother. Even after he blesses her ("O Russian faced, woman on the grass, your long black hair is crowned with flowers, the mandolin is on your knees ... / "O glorious muse that bore me from the womb, gave suck first mystic life and taught me talk and music ..."), the very next line reminds us she was "Tortured and beaten in the skull".

There is another tiny midrash that describes Naomi as a "remnant of remnant", and some of the most interesting of Ruth's afterlives appear in Pardes' epilogue, along with other "remainders" of her research. It is a little frustrating to read only glancing references to such rich topics as contemporary American groups of gleaners who collect farmers' surplus produce and donate it to people in need; Keats' haunting vision of Ruth "in tears amid the alien corn"; or the use of Ruth's oath in Jewish lesbian weddings. For all its breadth and occasional brilliance, this book left me wanting more.

Pinning down Joseph Roth

Mark Glanville

Endless Flight: The Life of Joseph Roth
Keiron Pim
Granta Books

To most readers, Joseph Roth's name is synonymous with *The Radetzky March*. It is certainly the Roth novel you are most likely to find in bookshops. Yet his oeuvre runs to six hefty volumes of fiction, short stories, journalism, letters and poems. To know *The Radetzky March*, though it is undoubtedly his masterpiece, is not to know the writer. Its length and perfection are not typical of his fiction. But as flawed as his lesser-known works can be, they sometimes pack a more powerful punch. In novels such as *Weights and Measures* and *The Legend of the Holy Drinker*, and in the journalism collected in *What I Saw: Reports from Berlin 1920–1933* and *The White Cities: Reports from France 1925–39*, there is a rawness, a directness and a very human imperfectness to enjoy. Roth's prose is always scintillating. He is now rightly regarded as one of the greatest writers of the twentieth century, yet many remain unfamiliar with his life and work. Keiron Pim's is the first full-length English biography of Joseph Roth, a long-awaited successor to Dennis Marks' brief but illuminating *Wandering Jew: The Search for Joseph Roth* (2011). There are two German biographies: Wilhelm von Sternburg's, published in 2009 and David Bronsen's in 1974, translated into French but not English. Fortunately, Roth has, in Pim, the finest advocate.

Joseph Roth maintained to some friends that he had been a lieutenant in the Austrian army during World War I and had won medals, one of which he enjoyed showing off; to another friend he confessed he had bought it from a junk dealer. He was never made a lieutenant. "He intentionally contradicts himself," writes Pim. "If you think you've placed him, he will prove you wrong." Pinning down such a protean character is no easy task. Roth's looseness with the facts of his life dovetailed with his spurning of the notion of objectivity, flying in the face of the trendy *Neue Sachlichkeit* (New Objectivity) movement of the interwar Weimar period, the German modern realism that was a reaction to Expressionism. In *Flight Without End* Roth claimed, "I have invented nothing, made up nothing. The question of 'poetic invention' is no longer relevant. Observed fact is all that counts." Yet in a letter written two years later, in 1929, he criticised the "objectivity" of another journalist, claiming, "my so-called subjectivity is in the highest degree objective. I can smell things he won't be able to see for another ten years."

Roth began his career as a poet (Nobel Prize–winning Russian poet Joseph Brodsky said that Roth had "a poem on every page"). His verdict on his idol, the poet Heinrich Heine – "Maybe he did make up the odd fact, but then he saw things the way they ought to be. His eye was more than visual apparatus and optic nerve" – applies equally well to Roth, as Michael Hofmann, his superlative translator and commentator, has pointed out. His poet's intuition made him quick to see the threat posed by the Nazis and, indeed, he was the first to allude to Hitler in a novel (his first, *The Spider's Web*, published in 1923). A newspaper editor encouraged him "to write not just poems but little stories too, for what he related orally was original and gripping", but it was the necessity of earning a living that propelled him into journalism. Nonetheless his prose, both in fiction and reportage, retained a poetic dimension: icicles hang from roofs "like tassels with rigor mortis"; "rains were soft, water in its most velvety form". Hofmann, on whom Pim – who has read Roth in English translation rather than the original German – sensibly relies, detects echoes of the great poet Rilke in the most unlikely areas of his journalism, such as an article entitled "Affirmation of the Triangular Railway Junction". Though the title reads like the header for a Soviet propaganda pamphlet, Roth celebrates the triumph of machine over man in Rilkean terms: "Here it is not passion that is omnipotent but regulation and law." Elsewhere, he describes the funeral of a soldier attended by veterans:

> Instead of the healthy, even rhythm of marching soldiers you could hear the uneven knocking of crutches on cobblestones, a music of wood and stone, mixed with the squeaking and creaking of artificial limbs ... There were cripples, whose faces were one gaping red hole, framed by white bandages, red scars instead of ears. There stood lumps of meat and blood, soldiers without any limbs, torsos in uniform.

This is not the work of a hack but the observations of a great writer who understands that monumental events are best evoked through their detail. Hofmann notes in his introduction to Roth's *What I Saw*, "It is a partial, and an interested, but to my mind a perfectly respectable opinion (held to by some readers and critics at the time) that Roth's masterpieces were not his novels but his feuilletons." The feuilleton, literally "small page", originated in early-nineteenth-century France. Described by Pim as "a lighter adjunct to political commentary", in that form Roth claimed to "paint the portrait of the age".

Roth produced coruscating prose in all media. But there is something profoundly Jewish at the heart of his writing. He was born in 1892 in Brody (then part of the Austro-Hungarian Empire and now in western Ukraine), sometime home of the Baal Shem Tov, founder of the mystical Hasidic movement. Hasidism, an alternative to the dry, law-based Judaism that had long been ascendant, was, at its peak, subscribed to by 90 per cent of Eastern European Jews. Roth's friend Géza von Cziffra noticed how "he would refer to the Hasidic belief in miracles held by the Orthodox Jews of his homeland, who saw logic as detrimental to faith". It is in his Jewishness that Pim, quoting the Polish-American rabbi Abraham Joshua Heschel on Talmudic commentators, locates another quality of Roth's: "Just as their thinking was distinguished by a reaching out for the most subtle, so their mode of expression, particularly that of those engaged in mystic lore, was marked by a tendency towards terseness."

For Roth, as for the great Romanian-Jewish poet Paul Celan, "German was literally the mother tongue", in whose language and literary tradition his genius had been moulded. The savage turning of German-speaking populations against the Jews created crises for both writers. Roth claimed that "German is a dead language"; Celan concluded that it was "gagged with the ashes of burnt-out meaning". After the war, Celan forged a German that served his poetic purpose: elliptical, archaic and obscure. Roth's answer was to retreat to a romanticised version of the Habsburg Empire into which he had been born, one that had fostered an internationalism in which many races and religions could thrive, a panacea against the destructive nationalism he saw enveloping Europe. For this reason, he was also a strong opponent of the nascent Zionist movement: "They are aping the recently failed European ideologies," he claimed. Theodor Herzl had once proposed mass baptism as the answer for Jews. Though it is not known whether Roth was ever baptised, he certainly embraced Catholicism, the religion of his beloved Habsburgs. According to Pim, "he identified France as a wellspring of that pan-European tolerant Catholic spirit which paralleled Judaism's transcendence of national borders and shamed Germany's aggressive insularity ... he saw Catholicism as a motor for the enrichment of European culture ... Catholicism seems a spiritual analogue for the supranational Habsburg Empire." Roth was never happier than when in France. "Nowhere does he write with such joy, nor such love for humanity," observes Pim.

Roth's fondness for the Habsburgs was also a function of his lifelong quest for father figures. He was an inveterate frequenter of hotels (*The Hotel Years*, translated and edited by Michael Hofmann in 2015, is a delightful collection of his journalism on the pains and pleasures of hotels and the deteriorating international situation of the 1930s). Pim writes poignantly of how Roth, ever on the lookout for paternal figures, found one in every hotel he visited. "The look with which the doorman welcomes me is more than a father's embrace," he wrote. Roth never knew his own father and was brought up by an uncle. "He must have been a strange man, an Austrian scallywag, a drinker and a spendthrift," writes Roth of the uncle. "He died insane when I was sixteen. His specialty was the melancholy which I inherited from him." The Habsburg emperor was another he enlisted into an abstract paternal role. Towards the end of his life, Roth even came to know the last one, Otto, who more than lived up to the altruistic, humanitarian qualities with which Roth had imbued his house. In 1940, Otto opposed Hitler and Mussolini and intervened to save the lives of thousands of French Jews. Alert to the alcoholism that was eventually to kill Roth, he also commanded, "Roth, I, as your Emperor, order you to cease drinking" – an order the writer disobeyed.

Earlier Habsburgs were not quite such *menschen*. In 1772, Empress Maria Theresa had declared, "In future no Jew shall be allowed to remain in Vienna without my special permission. I know of no greater plague than this race." Roth's relationship with his birthplace, Brody, and by extension the Eastern European Jew in him, was ambivalent. As with so much else in his life, he was in flight from both. Pim points out that Roth even used to claim he was born in nearby Schwaby, so as to place himself "within a German ethnic group known for their loyalty to Vienna and the Habsburgs". Though his marvellous, short 1927 book *The Wandering Jews* depicts, with considerable sympathy, a people tragically on the verge of destruction, Roth himself was tainted with the empress's prejudice. "Alas, my neighbour is a Jewess, and scares away my lime blossom with her appalling squawks. Her voice is shrill, and smells of onions," he lamented. Pim notes that Roth "knew well that antisemitic snobbery and hatred were internalised by Jews themselves: he saw it in western Jews' attitude to the *Ostjuden*, and in his own feelings about his Jewishness". Though he died in 1939, a year before his long-suffering, mentally ill wife Friedl was gassed in an *Aktion* – for her insanity, not her Judaism – he had seen enough to know where such attitudes led and was a consistently passionate anti-Nazi.

"He needs a little discomfort to feel alert," Pim observes, "too much comfort is soporific." There was little comfort in Roth's life but a good deal of pain – some, though not all, self-inflicted. In a portrait of Roth by Mies Blomsma, reproduced in the book, Roth praises the artist for capturing him so successfully: "Pissed off, soused but clever." Though he was always in flight, not all flights are bad. "Work is flight for me," he claimed. Roth told his great friend, the writer Stefan Zweig, "I think I can only understand the world when I'm writing, and the moment I put down my pen, I'm lost." Roth and Zweig's fascinating, bittersweet correspondence, much drawn on by Pim, is the centrepiece of Michael Hofmann's edition of Roth's letters. Over and above the Habsburgs, Catholicism and Judaism, writing was his true temple, and he was intolerant of its desecration at the hands of others, not least Zweig. At one point in their correspondence, Roth gives his frequent financial benefactor an exquisite masterclass in writing. Pim quotes an anecdote in which Roth is expelled from a hotel for blocking the lavatory. The reason? He had read a manuscript which "drove him into such a frenzied rage that he ripped it into pieces and tried to flush it down the toilet ... now workmen had had to be called in."

Pim, a first-class writer himself, rides the bucking bronco of his subject's life expertly, allowing the reader to stay with Roth through all his mutations and incarnations. It is a brilliant achievement. At the end of the book we feel we have come to know Roth, his circle of family and acquaintances and the various locations and milieux in which he operated, as well as the work itself (all of the novels are treated to detailed, critical analysis). In his sympathy with Roth and absorption in his life, Pim has produced a biography of a great writer utterly worthy of its subject. Everyone interested in writing and writers should read this fine work of literature. ≣

Past issues

"For a long time now, the authority of knowledge has been under siege from those who march under the banner of pure belief."
—Simon Schama

The Return of History investigates rising global populism, and the forces propelling modern nativism and xenophobia.

"Traditional principles and allegiances have given way to realpolitik." —Lina Khatib

The New Middle East examines the dramatic changes unfolding in the region as new rivalries, blocs and partnerships are formed – based not on ideology but on pragmatism.

"The left has become the ideology that dare not speak its name." —Anshel Pfeffer

In *The Strange Death and Curious Rebirth of the Israeli Left*, Anshel Pfeffer takes the pulse of Israel's left wing, examining its health and prospects and dissecting the country's complex post-Netanyahu political reality.

"If ink on paper can reassemble a world …"
—Rachel Kadish

The Jewish world of pre-war Europe was almost destroyed. If we hold up a lantern to that darkness, what can we discover about what was lost, what survived and what could have been?

"Younger writers were freed to think about specifically Jewish questions. [Their] work has a narrower appeal. Only time will tell if it is also a deeper one." —Adam Kirsch

After the Golden Age examines the current generation of leading American Jewish writers as they grapple with questions about religion, Israel, politics and multiculturalism.

"Iran's strategy is to eat away at American power, while legitimising its own role as a regional power with nuclear ambitions." —Kim Ghattas

Iran examines the motivations behind the country's changing role and influence in the Middle East, delving into the regime's secretive strategy and tactics.

"The process of saying goodbye to these two authors, who had been a visible presence in Israeli society for decades, is far from over."
—Nir Baram

The Pen and the Sword explores the efforts by successive generations of Israeli writers to grapple with their nation's difficult political questions.

"Ukrainians voted for a mixture of Benny Hill and Boris Johnson, and they somehow wound up with Churchill."
—Vladislav Davidzon

The Jews of Ukraine explores the rich, tumultuous history of the Jews of Ukraine, who have played a pivotal role in modern Jewish life.

Add these past issues to your subscription when buying online.

Subscribe to The Jewish Quarterly and save.

Enjoy free delivery of The Jewish Quarterly to your door, digital access to every issue of The Jewish Quarterly for one year, and exclusive special offers.

Forthcoming issue:
JQ253: *Ivrit* (August 2023)

Never miss an issue.
Subscribe and save.

- 1 year* print and digital subscription (4 issues) £42 GBP | $56 USD
- 1 year* digital subscription (4 issues) £25 GBP | $32 USD

Subscribe now:
Visit jewishquarterly.com/subscribe
Email subscribe@jewishquarterly.com

Scan one of these QR codes with your mobile device camera app:

Subscribe in £GBP   Subscribe in $USD

PRICES INCLUDE POSTAGE AND HANDLING.
Prices and discounts current at the time of printing. We also offer subscriptions in AUD for subscribers from Australia, New Zealand and Asia, and for existing subscribers to Schwartz Media titles. See our website for more information. *Your subscription will automatically renew until you notify us to stop. We will send you a reminder notice prior to the end of your subscription period.

www.ingramcontent.com/pod-product-compliance
Lightning Source LLC
Chambersburg PA
CBHW020713200426
43197CB00061B/1461